Don’t Be Canada

Don't Be Canada

How One Country
Did Everything Wrong
All At Once

Tristin Hopper

TORONTO, 2025

Sutherland House
416 Moore Ave., Suite 304
Toronto, ON M4G 1C9

First edition, March 2025

If you are interested in inviting one of our authors to a live event or media appearance, please contact sranasinghe@sutherlandhousebooks.com and visit our website at sutherlandhousebooks.com for more information.

We acknowledge the support of the Government of Canada.

Manufactured in Canada
Cover designed by Luisa Galstyan and Jordan Lunn

Library and Archives Canada Cataloguing in Publication
Title: Don't be Canada : how one country did everything wrong all at once / Tristin Hopper.
Names: Hopper, Tristin, author.
Description: Includes bibliographical references.
Identifiers: Canadiana (print) 20250124297 | Canadiana (ebook) 20250124386 | ISBN 9781998365364 (softcover) | ISBN 9781998365371 (EPUB)
Subjects: LCSH: World politics—21st century. | LCSH: Canada—Foreign relations—21st century. | CSH: Canada—Politics and government—2015-
Classification: LCC FC642 .H67 2025 | DDC 327.71—dc23

ISBN 978-1-998365-36-4
eBook 978-1-998365-37-1

To Allison

Contents

Introduction

The Country that Didn't Work Anymore

In spring 2023, the UK House of Commons convened a series of committee hearings to explore how they might institute a system of legal euthanasia.

Polls had long showed more than two-thirds of Britons favouring some kind of legal doctor-assisted suicide, but before Parliamentarians put pen to paper on any kind of legislation, they held a full inquiry to explore what such a system might look like. The assembled British MPs heard from bioethicists, hospital directors, and foreign experts. They even took a field trip to the US state of Oregon to see a legal euthanasia program in action.[1]

One theme was clear: whatever the British decided to do about euthanasia, they should make sure that it was as far as possible from whatever Canada had done. "I would say that Canada is a warning sign for countries that legalize medical assistance in dying," University of Toronto bioethicist Trudo Lemmens told the parliamentarians.[2] Another witness would call the Canadian system "disturbing."[3]

It's not just Canada's approach to euthanasia that foreigners are finding disturbing. In April 2024, HBO host Bill Maher opened his show with a ten-minute dissection of how Canada wasn't the progressive utopia that Americans seemed to think it was. "There's only one problem with thinking everything's better in Canada; it's not. Not anymore, anyway," he said.[4]

Maher, a lifelong progressive, called Canada a "cautionary tale" of what happens when a country goes too far left. "They say in politics, liberals are the gas pedal, and conservatives are the brakes, and I'm generally with the gas pedal, but not if we're driving off a cliff," he said.

In May 2024 the New York-based Rockefeller Foundation issued a public warning to beware of the fate of the "breakdown nations."[5] These were defined as countries who had once been star performers in the world economy, but were now locked into both political and economic decline.

At the top of the list was Canada. Rockefeller Foundation chair Ruchir Sharma wrote that whatever private investment still existed in Canada was mostly being used to bid up real estate, with job growth "being driven mainly by the government."

"Pressed to name a digital success, Canadians cite Shopify—but the online store is the only tech name among the country's ten largest companies, and its shares are trading at half their 2021 peak," he added.

Canada is now topping the charts on any number of inglorious indicators. *The Telegraph* has declared Vancouver the "fentanyl capital of the world."[6] *The Times* has branded Canada the "world capital of assisted dying."[7] The BBC has pegged Canada as "a car theft capital of the world."[8]

Canada now has one of the lowest birth rates on the planet, joining a "lowest low" club that includes South Korea, Spain, Italy, and Japan. And Canada got there pretty quickly; fertility rates have plummeted in only a few years due almost entirely to economic factors.[9] According to federal research, the average Canadian couple wants to have as many kids as the average American family, but they can't afford it.[10]

The Canadian archetype of the thriving, grateful immigrant has now been replaced with web forums filled with newcomers expressing regret at ever having come. Russia's all-out invasion of Ukraine in 2022 prompted a wave of Ukrainian refugees into Canada, home to one of the world's largest Ukrainian diaspora communities. Almost as quickly as they arrived, they decided to become economic refugees from Canada. "I'm tired all the time now," Oleksii Martynenko told Bloomberg News in a 2023 interview.[11] "I want to go back to Europe because it's such a difficult life in Canada."

In early 2024, BBC's India bureau profiled how the end of the "Canadian dream" was spurring a reverse migration of Punjabis to their home state.[12] "Everything was so expensive. I had to work 50 hours every week after college, just to survive," said one, identified as a twenty-eight-year-old named Balkar.

Canada's official guide for new immigrants is now an exercise in managing expectations.[13] "Most Canadians spend 35 percent to 50 percent of their income on housing and utilities," it reads, adding that they can save on furniture and clothes by shopping at second-hand stores.

Of late, whenever Canada has garnered international attention on the world stage, it's often been for something humiliating.

Canada was among the single worst performers during the 2021 scramble to evacuate Kabul in advance of its takeover by the Taliban. The Canadian airlift started late, ended early, and featured ignominious scenes of former interpreters for the Canadian military being asked to brave Taliban checkpoints to make it to the airport—only for them to be abandoned anyway.[14]

When the Canadian Parliament had the rare honour of hosting wartime Ukrainian President Volodymyr Zelenskyy, they immediately stumbled into the near-unbelievable international scandal of holding a standing ovation for a ninety-eight-year-old veteran of the Waffen-SS.

The nonagenarian's family had introduced him as a Second World War veteran who had "fought the Russians," and nobody on Parliament Hill thought this sounded suspicious. Poland reacted by demanding the man's immediate extradition for war crimes.[15]

At a 2023 G20 summit in New Delhi, Canada's participation was mostly remembered for the fact that their official plane broke down at the airport, prompting Indian Prime Minister Narendra Modi to reportedly rub it in just a little by offering them his own plane to get home.[16]

* * *

It was not too long ago that Canada's internal workings were famously uninteresting to the non-Canadian world. In the 1980s, the US journalist Michael Kinsley declared that the most boring headline ever written was a *New York Times* column entitled "Worthwhile Canadian initiative."

"Election night in Canada has no major problems as 13 million paper ballots counted by hand," was the headline on the Associated Press' requisite story about the 2000 Canadian federal election.

After Quebec narrowly voted down an independence referendum in 1995, *Washington Post* columnist Charles Krauthammer penned an ode to "dependable, boring Canada; the Canada that Americans so safely ignore."

By contrast, the Canada of the 2020s has come to rival Florida and Japan in its ability to inspire a near-constant stream of ridiculous or unbelievable news stories.

When the world's health authorities were scrambling to publish social distancing guidelines in the first months of COVID-19 lockdowns, it was only Canada where these guidelines included a suggestion to consider employing "glory holes," a hole in a wall intended to facilitate anonymous sex. "Use barriers, like walls (e.g., glory holes), that allow for sexual contact but prevent close face-to-face contact," read guidelines published by the British Columbia Centre for Disease Control.[17]

When the Canadian federal government tabled a seemingly routine bill to combat "online harms" in early 2024, legal scholars around the world were soon noting that it prescribed life sentences for speech offences and even included provisions to pre-emptively detain citizens if there was a "reasonable belief" to suspect they might say something hateful in future.

"Canada considers life sentences for offending someone based off sex, age, or race," was the headline on Sky News Australia.[18] Amnesty International even got involved, declaring that Canada was flirting with "disproportionate punishments that risk chilling legitimate speech."[19]

The Canadian Cancer Society inspired headlines as far away as India when it apologized for using the word "cervix" in its literature about cervical cancer. "You may prefer other words, such as 'front hole,'" it read.[20]

It was at a 2023 women's meet by the Canadian Powerlifting Union that a bearded competitor showed up, utterly shattered the record for the women's bench press, and then went right back to identifying as a man as soon as the result was logged. "Man enters powerlifter competition as woman, breaks record," declared the *New York Post*. As this book goes to press, the record still stands.[21]

And the headlines bring us back to euthanasia. Whenever some foreign publication profiles an example of a system gone mad, it's almost always about Canada:

- Welcome to Canada, the Doctor Will Kill You Now (*Wall Street Journal*, September 2024)
- Now Canada is euthanising autistic people (Spiked Online, March 2024)
- Canada moves one step closer to euthanizing children (*Daily Mail*, February 2023)
- The Canadian State Is Euthanizing Its Poor and Disabled (Jacobin, May 2024)
- More than a quarter of Canadians think homelessness, poverty are reasons for assisted suicide (Fox News, May 2023)

This has been happening so often that even the jokes about Canada have changed. After decades of being synonymous with blandness and free health care, Canada is now comedic shorthand as the place that kills its sick and infirm. One widely circulated meme shows a stick figure seeking attention for a cut requiring stitches.[22] The US doctor hands him a bill for $58,000, the British doctor promises to help him "in 38 months," and the Canadian simply declares "kill yourself."

Or there's this December 2022 headline from the Florida-based satirical news site The Babylon Bee: "Canadian Doctor Loses License For Not Wearing Mask While Euthanizing Patient."

Canadians are well aware there's something wrong, even if they struggle to define precisely what it is. The polling agency Ipsos celebrated Canada Day 2024 with a survey noting that 70 percent of the populace agreed that

Canada was "broken."[23] A different survey by pollster Leger found the exact same result; seven in ten agreed with the statement "it feels like everything is broken in this country right now."[24]

Within this new morass of national dissatisfaction, there are political forces taking place in Canada that are unlike anything else in the Western world. Whole demographics of Canadians that never used to touch right-wing politics with a ten-foot pole are now completely in the tank for conservative parties. Women, union members, poor people, immigrants; all these demographics are now routinely telling pollsters that the Conservatives are their favourite party.[25] Canada is now one of the world's only democratic countries where young people are supporting Conservative candidates at rates well beyond that of their parents.

When forty-four-year-old Pierre Poilievre became leader of the Conservative Party of Canada in 2023, pollster David Coletto was shocked to see data showing that Poilievre's popularity was the strongest among Canadians under the age of thirty-four. "If someone told me that the Conservative leader would be MORE popular with younger Canadians than older ones a few years ago, I'd tell you were nuts," he wrote in a social media post.[26]

Call it extreme progressivism, call it political correctness, call it wokeness, call it post-nationalism, or call it post-modernism: whatever it is, Canada has been getting it harder and faster than anyone else. And for the most part, Canadians are not liking what they see.

This book is about how one of the richest, most tolerant and most functional countries on earth decided to take wealth, tolerance, and functionality for granted. It's about how the most educated nation on earth was convinced to go all-out on unproven theories without considering the consequences.

If you're a Canadian, this is a cursory history of how it came to be that there's a crack pipe vending machine at your local hospital, why the men's bathroom at the army base has a tampon dispenser, and why the brochure for your mom's nursing home includes a hotline to call if she's "thinking about medical assistance in dying."

If you're not a Canadian, this is a guide on how you might steer clear of those things. And if you're a Canadian reading this in the future, this is a guide on how not to do those things again.

There is a lot of human tragedy in the coming pages: whole generations robbed of potential, scores of preventable deaths, and untold numbers of innocent people caught within the wheels of a terrifying Kafkaesque bureaucracy.

But I'm not going to pretend that Canada's descent into madness isn't simultaneously one of the most darkly comic things a country has ever done to itself. Nobody will fault you if you laugh.

1 | The Easiest Country to Get Euthanasia'ed

When Canada first legalized assisted suicide, which it officially refers to as "medical assistance in dying" (MAID), the official estimate was that it would be rare, only ever used as a last resort.

In 2018, when Health Canada began stockpiling the lethal substances that would underlie the new MAID system, they calculated their orders based on "the assumption that Canada would reach a steady state of 2.05 percent of total deaths attributed to medical assistance in dying."[1] Given that Canada had recorded 276,689 total deaths in 2017, this worked out to a maximum of about 6,000 MAID deaths per year.

When a team of Canadian health researchers tried to estimate what impact MAID would have on organ donation, they were even more conservative in their forecasts. Once Canadians had access to MAID, they assumed that it would rise to a maximum of about five euthanasia cases each day. "Approximately 2000 euthanasia cases are expected in Canada each year," read their report, published in the *New England Journal of Medicine*.[2]

Neither of those estimates was even close to correct.

By 2020, Canadian MAID deaths had already soared to an annual total of 7,611.[3] The next year, they hit 10,064. By 2021, so many were dying of MAID that the Province of Quebec alone blew past The Netherlands as the world's leader in physician-assisted death.[4] By 2022, one in every twenty-five Canadian deaths was by assisted suicide.[5] Every single year since MAID has been made legal, it has grown by about 30 percent, and that rise has shown no sign of slowing down.

The spike has been so beyond anyone's expectations that when Canada's official heath agency tried to predict when MAID deaths would level off, it was proved wrong within a matter of months. Buried within a May 2022 batch of federal government cost estimates was the projection that MAID mortality would only reach 4 percent of total deaths by 2033, after eleven years of "steady state growth."[6] Instead, Canada reached the milestone within the year; 4.1 percent of Canadians died of MAID in 2022.

Nothing like this has happened before. As of 2024, fourteen countries have some form of legal physician-assisted suicide. And not one of the other thirteen has seen assisted suicide deaths rise anywhere near as quickly as they have in Canada.

The US state of California, with about the same population as Canada, first legalized assisted dying in June 2016, right around the time of Canada's MAID law. In 2022, only 853 Californians died of what they call "aid-in-dying." That same year, 13,241 Canadians died of MAID, over fifteen times more.[7]

Within Canada's cascade of unexpected MAID cases has come a whole litany of scandals.[8] Prior to MAID, it was The Netherlands and Belgium that were furnishing most of the world's major headlines about the extremes of assisted suicide. In 2013, new outlets across Canada carried the story of Marc and Eddy Verbessem, blind Belgian twins who were approved to die at age forty-five because they had started to go deaf.[9] Canada is now the poster child for what happens when a country becomes drunk on easy euthanasia.

There was the Alberta father who went to court to try to halt the scheduled assisted suicide of his twenty-seven-year-old mentally ill daughter. The daughter, identified only as M.V., suffered from autism and severe ADHD. In court, the father argued that the physical symptoms that had qualified M.V. for MAID likely didn't exist and were instead the result of "undiagnosed psychological conditions." The court didn't litigate whether that was true, but it did determine that the father had no legal right to obstruct the medical autonomy of his daughter. In the words of M.V.'s lawyers, the father did not have "the right to keep her alive against her wishes."[10]

In 2002, a caseworker at Veterans Affairs was found repeatedly offering death to ex-soldiers, including those with PTSD.[11] Another veteran, former Paralympian Christine Gauthier, went public with her experience of requesting a home wheelchair lift and instead being offered MAID: "I have a letter saying that if you're so desperate, madam, we can offer you MAID, medical assistance in dying," Gauthier told a Parliamentary committee.[12]

A Canadian justice system that executed its last criminal in 1962 is now doing so again, provided the offender makes a MAID request first. In 2023, it first emerged that the Canadian prison system had begun carrying out assisted suicide on prisoners, with the inmates typically remaining shackled throughout the procedure.[13] Ivan Zinger, the Correctional Investigator of Canada, has repeatedly told legislators that Canada is the only country that does this. In one report, Zinger even detailed the case of an inmate who was approved for MAID mostly because he kept threatening suicide.

Roger Foley, an Ontario man hospitalized with a degenerative brain disorder, recorded hospital staff badgering him to seek MAID in order to save the hospital money. On the tape, Foley turned over to the US-based Associated Press, the hospital's director of ethics can be heard saying that it would cost "north of $1,500 a day" to keep him alive and asking whether he "had an interest in assisted dying."[14]

When another foreign news service, Reuters, profiled the Canadian MAID system in the summer 2023, it found a forty-seven-year-old woman with anorexia whose desire for death would soon meet the federal threshold for assisted suicide. "Every day is hell. I'm so tired. I'm done. I've tried everything," said Lisa Pauli.[15]

A 2024 BBC documentary on assisted suicide entitled *Better Off Dead?* would become most notable for an unsettling interview with Ellen Wiebe, a Canadian MAID practitioner. Wiebe, who has administered MAID about 400 times, was interviewed by British Liz Carr, who uses a wheelchair due to a rare joint disability. When Carr asks if a person like herself would be able to legally end their life in Canada, Wiebe replied with a laugh "Liz, right now, you love life and you want to live, but there's lots of nasty illnesses you might get."

Against Carr's assertion that Canada's program could be putting disabled people at fatal risk, Wiebe said that the only alternative is "condemning others to suffering, unbearable suffering."

"I am so glad—so glad—that I'm a Canadian and that we have this law so that people can choose that, or not choose that," she added.

Scott Kim is a bioethics investigator at the US National Institutes of Health and a vocal critic of Canada's low-barrier approach to assisted dying. In an interview for this book, he described attending an assisted dying roundtable where "a Canadian academic seriously raised the question 'you know, do you think poverty could be considered an irremediable condition that qualifies them [for MAID]?' And my thought was 'how can you even propose that as a topic of discussion?' But it didn't seem to shock people at the table."

* * *

Two years before a single Canadian had died of a doctor-assisted suicide, the Angus Reid Institute asked Canadians what they thought about euthanasia. The results of the 2014 poll were overwhelming; 79 percent favoured allowing Canadian doctors to "assist with the suicide of their patients by prescribing lethal drugs."[16]

Similar proportions believed that Canadians should be allowed the option of assisted suicide if they have a terminal illness (82 percent) or were in a "great deal of pain" (76 percent).

And this has stayed pretty consistent. The Canadian consensus, then and now, is that Canadians who are imminently dying or in extreme pain should be allowed to punch out early at a time of their choosing.

If the Canadian experiment with assisted suicide deviated almost immediately from a wish for a "dignified" end, much of that blame can be placed on a single court decision. Canada's MAID era began on February 6, 2015, with the release of Carter v. Canada, a Supreme Court decision that struck down the country's existing ban on assisted suicide. Prior to then, the Canadian Criminal Code has prescribed prison terms of up to fourteen years for anyone who "aids or abets a person to commit suicide."

The Carter case, despite its name, had been set in motion by Gloria Taylor, a BC woman who had been diagnosed with ALS, popularly known as Lou Gehrig's Disease. Facing a slow and painful end from the degenerative illness, Taylor had gone to court, asserting that it was her constitutional right to obtain a physician-assisted death. "I do not want to die slowly, piece by piece. I do not want to waste away unconscious in a hospital bed," she testified.[17] Rather, she wanted a "dignified good-bye."

But the Supreme Court took it even further, ruling that anybody with a "grievous and irremediable medical condition" could also be a candidate for euthanasia. To do otherwise would be a violation of the constitutionally guaranteed right to "life, liberty and security of the person." That's one of the more surreal arguments that appear in the Carter decision: assisted death is necessary in order to protect Canadians' "right to life."

The reasoning was that by banning assisted suicide, Taylor might be compelled "to take her life earlier than she otherwise would if she had access to a physician-assisted death." In other words, to prevent Canadians from killing themselves, the government needed to give them a wider berth to kill themselves.

The court placed vanishingly few limits on how all this assisted suicide would take place: if a Canadian could prove "suffering that is intolerable to the individual," they were now constitutionally cleared to seek death. The decision even argued that such top-level safeguards were unnecessary, since the system would probably work fine. "We should not lightly assume that the regulatory regime will function defectively, nor should we assume that other criminal sanctions against the taking of lives will prove impotent against abuse," it read.

Weirdly, the Carter decision came just two decades after the Supreme Court dealt with a near-identical case and declared that assisted suicide was none of its business. In 1993, the court heard Rodriguez v. British Columbia. Sue Rodriguez, forty-two, had been diagnosed with ALS, the same disease as Lee Taylor, and was seeking the same thing: the legal right to "by her own hand, at the time of her choosing, end her life."

Rodriguez's argument was exactly the same as the one in Carter. By placing a blanket ban on physician-assisted suicide, Rodriguez argued that Canada was violating her right to "life, liberty and security of the person."

The court wasn't unsympathetic to Rodriguez's plight. As the case progressed, the justices had witnessed her visibly deteriorating condition first-hand. "I have the deepest sympathy for the appellant and her family, as I am sure do all of my colleagues, and I am aware that the denial of her application by this Court may prevent her from managing the manner of her death," wrote Justice John Sopinka.[18] But in a 5-4 decision, the justices ultimately concluded that it didn't violate the Constitution for Canada to maintain a ban on assisted suicide, and it wasn't even that unreasonable: "Given the concerns about abuse and the great difficulty in creating appropriate safeguards, the blanket prohibition on assisted suicide is not arbitrary or unfair."

The Supreme Court of 2015 didn't have a great answer for why it had suddenly come to the opposite conclusion only twenty-two years later in the Carter decision. The Constitution hadn't changed in the interim, nor had the Criminal Code clause, which banned assisted suicide. But the later judges wrote that "the matrix of legislative and social facts" was different, as was Canada's "legal conception" of its Constitution.

By declaring that any "grievous and irremediable medical condition" was grounds for a doctor-assisted death, the Supreme Court had effectively thwarted any future attempt Canada would make to keep assisted suicide on a leash.

The Carter decision gave Parliament one year to figure out what Canada's new MAID regime would look like. And lawmakers considered every conceivable demographic in their subsequent deliberations, from sick children to the mentally ill to the severely disabled. The result was Bill C-14, a piece of legislation designed to strike an "appropriate balance" between the "autonomy" of Canadians seeking an early death and "the interests of vulnerable persons and of society."

The signature measures of Bill C-14 were that, in Canada, assisted suicide could only be responsibly offered to terminally ill Canadians over the age of eighteen and only those suffering adults whose death was "reasonably foreseeable."

The whole process was a model of parliamentary cooperation; the bill had been preceded by months of hearings and public consultations. When Bill C-14 came up for debate in the House of Commons, MPs from all of Canada's major parties found something to like about it and were deliberately polite and nonpartisan in their language. "No one here is wrong, no one here is right. We are all honest Canadians and we want to do what is best for the future of this country and for the future of Canadians," declared Conservative MP Gérard Deltell.

And then, within just three years, a single Quebec judge put all of it through a shredder.

In 2019, Justice Christine Baudouin of the Quebec Superior Court quashed Bill-14, saying it was unconstitutional and even discriminatory. By deciding that only the terminally ill are deserving of euthanasia, the law denied other Canadians who want to die "equal recognition of their human dignity."

Once again, the court pulled out the same argument that Canadians' charter right to life gave them a right to death, since any stricture on Canadians legally ending their lives would only drive them to do it illegally. "The reasonably foreseeable natural death requirement thus exposes individual … to a heightened risk of death," read the decision.[19]

The case had surrounded Jean Truchon, a fifty-one-year-old Quebec man with a host of degenerative illnesses that had rendered him paralyzed, suffering from intense chronic pain, and deeply depressed. Court documents are replete with testimony from Truchon detailing the ways he had considered ending his life, including driving his wheelchair in front of a bus, drowning himself, overdosing on illicit street drugs, or simply starving himself (and he vowed that if he lost the case, he would fall back on the latter). Yet the decision quotes from a medical expert claiming "Mr. Truchon is not suicidal, despite his wish to die."

The federal government refused to challenge the Baudouin decision, even though disability rights advocates had begged it to appeal to the Supreme Court. In a 2019 open letter co-signed by seventy other organizations, the Canadian Council for People with Disabilities warned that the Truchon decision risked ushering in a regime of disabled Canadians being pressured into early death.[20] "Canadians with disabilities are already bombarded daily with reminders that they are unwelcome and under-valued," it wrote. "We must not compound this harm by entrenching in law the message that others who share their condition will receive our full support if they choose to die prematurely."

The letter went unheeded. Justice Minister David Lametti instead proposed a new law, Bill C-7, that not only dropped terminal illness as a requirement for assisted suicide but also slashed many of the practice's prior safeguards. A MAID application previously required two independent witnesses; now just one. Under the prior law, you couldn't euthanize someone who had dropped into a coma or become mentally incompetent. Now you could, provided the patient had been approved for MAID beforehand. "For Canadians who are suffering intolerably, this process has taken too long, but their wait is now over," declared Lametti.

This time around, the bill absolutely did not have all-party support. Conservatives and the NDP (Canada's equivalent of Labour) all voted against it, and it passed in 2021 by just 180 out of 338 votes in the House of Commons.

This was also the bill that approved the extension of assisted suicide to Canadians whose only underlying condition was mental illness. As per C-7, anything from depression to bipolar disorder to PTSD was grounds for a legal death, provided the patient said it was "grievous and irremediable." Only weeks before its implementation, Ottawa delayed it until 2027 on the grounds that Canadian doctors were "not yet ready," a rare step back on the country's headlong euthanasia rush.[21]

Meanwhile, Canada's influential coterie of MAID activists have been open about their intention to keep pushing until assisted suicide is opened up to ever broader frontiers of Canadians.

At the heart of Canada's entire MAID regime is a single lobby group: Dying with Dignity. It was influential in pressing the Carter decision to the Supreme Court and in pushing forward the Truchon case. It has also been at the elbow of Canadian regulators in drawing up the country's MAID procedures. In many cases, it is the regulator.

Dying With Dignity shares significant overlap with the Canadian Association of MAID Assessors and Providers, a group that was given $3.3 million by the federal government to provide MAID training to Canadian health care practitioners.[22]

Soon after Ottawa delayed the mental illness provision, Dying with Dignity's lawyers challenged it in court.[23] As in the other cases, the argument is that obstructing Canadians' access to death is a violation of their charter-guaranteed right to life.

Dying With Dignity is actively championing the extension of MAID to "mature minors," a category it defines as anyone "at least 12 years of age and capable of making decisions with respect to their health."

"As with adults, there should be a presumption of capacity for these minors," reads a Dying with Dignity blog post on the topic.[24] The organization has never actually specified at what threshold it would consider assisted death to be inappropriate.

In a 2024 feature for *The Walrus* magazine, Dying with Dignity CEO Helen Long was asked whether her organization would ever go so far as to favour a future in which minors were eligible for assisted suicide solely on the basis of mental illness.[25] "I mean, that's so far down the road," she said. "I don't know." In that same interview, she added, "as far as we're concerned, there is no evidence that MAID has been delivered inappropriately."

If Dying with Dignity has been instrumental in transforming Canada into a mecca of hyper-liberalized euthanasia, what's most remarkable is how easy it was. The group has only fourteen full-time staff members and receives about $2 million in donations per year.[26] Much of its most influential advocacy was secured by a single $7 million donation made by Vancouver entrepreneur David Jackson in 2018. Dying With Dignity called the donation "transformational."[27]

Compare that to the $200 million per year that is needed to run the National Rifle Association, the usual analogue for an all-powerful lobby group.[28] Or how the price tag on a single US Senate race will routinely top $100 million.[29]

Canada has turned into a global mecca for low-barrier assisted suicide in record time and for about the price of a Super Bowl ad. "It was a very organized effort to push for legalization of MAID in Canada, with groundwork that was carefully laid (by people) who truly understood how the system works, and it totally caught the non-advocacy crowd by surprise," said Scott Kim.

In terms of the raw legality surrounding assisted suicide, Canada is still not quite as liberal as some of its European cousins. The Swiss, famously, have almost no laws whatsoever regulating euthanasia. Ever since 1940, the Swiss penal code's only check on assisted suicide is that it can't be done for "selfish motives." And even then, the maximum penalty is just five years in jail.

What has arguably made the Canadian system more aggressive than others is how assisted suicide has been incorporated into the health care system as just another form of treatment. Canada's forty-six-page "model guidance document" for MAID tells health care workers that it their duty to bring up assisted suicide as a treatment option.[30]

The document tells Canada's doctors and nurse practitioners that they must "take reasonable steps to ensure persons are informed of the full range of treatment options available to relieve suffering." As per the model guidance, if a patient isn't bringing up MAID on their own, it's unethical to assume that it's simply because they don't want it. Doctors and nurses "must not assume all persons potentially eligible for MAID are aware that MAID is legal and available in Canada."

The Canadian Association of MAID Assessors and Providers has a fourteen-page policy document telling clinicians of their "professional obligation" to bring up MAID as a "clinical care option."[31] It reads: "When a patient is potentially eligible, not providing them with information about MAID can create a significant risk of harm to them and their family."

Kim said that all the other countries offering physician-assisted suicide treat it as a civil rights issue. It might be administered via the health care system, but it exists as an entirely separate legal entity. "Nobody, prior to Canada, thought 'this is a medical good,' " said Kim. Rather than being approached as an unspoken last resort, Kim said the Canadian system has embraced MAID as if it's "a new treatment that's been invented by the Canadian Supreme Court."

This sentiment goes well beyond the walls of Canada's hospitals and clinics. All throughout Canadian civil society, there are now instances of assisted suicide being treated as just another form of palliative care. If you move an elderly relative into a care home operated by the BC government, you'll now be handed a brochure outlining the facility's various MAID options. "Eligibility assessments for MAID are available at all care homes … do ask if your care home offers the full MAID services," reads the official Resident and Family Handbook for the BC long-term care system.[32] It includes a hotline to reach the nearest "MAID coordination center."

Conversely, several major Canadian disability nonprofits have begun reassuring their clients that they won't be offered MAID. "This organization will not recommend, suggest, or refer anyone to Medical Assistance in Dying as an alternative to assisting in obtaining necessary supports and services that you require," reads a poster circulated by the group Disability Without Poverty.[33]

* * *

Canadian health researchers have begun openly celebrating the fact that MAID has resulted in a boon of organ and tissue donation. Canada now leads the world in the niche category of organ donation after euthanasia. A 2021 Dutch paper on organ donation after euthanasia found 286 instances of the practice worldwide, of which 136 were Canadian. "It's a wonderful opportunity for someone facing death to make something significant out of the end of their life," was how Arthur Schafer, director of the University of Manitoba's Centre for Professional and Applied Ethics, described the trend to CTV.[34]

MAID's even started to work its way into health budgeting. When Ottawa broadened MAID access to Canadians who weren't terminally ill, its Parliamentary Budget Officer was ordered to draw up an analysis of how much the new measures would cost. The startlingly clinical result was a seventeen-page report concluding that MAID expansion would provide net savings to the Canadian taxpayer. The measures would result in another 1,164 MAID deaths in the coming calendar year at a cost of $4.4 million, while the elimination of all these patients would represent a $66.5 million savings to the health care system. The "incremental net reduction in costs" of the expanded MAID regime was about $62 million per year. "To conclude, expanding access to MAID will result in a net reduction in health care costs for the provincial governments," wrote the report.[35]

Canada cannot claim that it wasn't given ample warning that a poorly designed euthanasia regime could very quickly go off the rails. During the hearings for Carter s. Canada, the Supreme Court heard from a Belgian bioethicist, Etienne Montero, who eerily predicted how the coming years were to play out. "Strict safeguards" were an illusion, he told the court. "Once euthanasia is allowed, it becomes very difficult to maintain a strict interpretation of the statutory conditions," he warned.

The Canadian justices dismissed Montero as the emissary of "a very different medico-legal culture."

Those at the front lines of the Canadian MAID system have been open about the fact that assisted suicide is rapidly becoming a quick fix employed in lieu of more complex treatments.

Madeline Li runs the MAID program for University Health Network, which operates four hospitals in the Toronto area. In a 2023 column for *Maclean's* magazine, Li described a patient who was applying for MAID due to depression and suicidality.[36] "The patient told me that if they didn't feel quite as lonely, if they felt that anyone cared about them at all, they probably could tolerate their pain better," she wrote.

Li tried to get the patient into a psychotherapy program but was unsuccessful. As such, MAID once again rose to the top of the list for potential treatment options. "I have no doubt in my mind that when they apply, they could be found eligible and receive it," she wrote.

Canada's rapid embrace of assisted suicide has also dispensed with any number of safeguards present in other jurisdictions. Eleven of fifty US states offer some form of legal assisted suicide, and they've all generally steered clear of the scandals and skyrocketing case rates experienced by Canada. This is largely thanks to two simple checks: patients have to be terminally ill, and they have to administer the fatal drugs themselves. Neither safeguard applies in Canada.

Belgium and The Netherlands both have independent commissions to oversee their assisted suicide regimes, collect data, and investigate abuse. In Canada, the entire program is run through the same federal health body as any other medical procedure. Most countries with assisted suicide require the approval of at least one doctor. In Belgium, it's three doctors; the attending physician and two others, one of whom must be a psychiatrist. In Canada, the entire process can be completed with nurse practitioners. A patient makes a written request and if two nurse practitioners sign off, it's approved. If either of those two nurse practitioners says "no," the patient can shop around until they find a nurse willing to say "yes."

The aforementioned Ellen Wiebe described doing exactly that in a recorded seminar of the Canadian Association of MAiD Assessors and Providers. The recording was noted in a 2022 expose by writer Alexander Raikin.

Wiebe related how she was in touch with a man who'd been rejected for MAID on two counts; he didn't have a serious illness and lacked the "capacity to make informed decisions." As Wiebe describes it, "he flew all by himself to Vancouver … I picked him up at the airport, um, brought him to my clinic and provided for him."[37]

In New Zealand and the parts of Australia that offer assisted dying, it is illegal for health providers to suggest euthanasia to a patient in their care. "The (patient) must be the one to raise assisted dying with someone in their health care team. Health professionals cannot suggest it as an option," reads Health New Zealand's official guidelines on assisted dying.[38] In Canada, as mentioned, it's not only legal for health providers to suggest euthanasia as a treatment, but it's a recommended medical practice.

In lieu of any number of guardrails that could have kept MAID on a tighter leash, Canada's main tack has been to repeatedly declare that there is nothing to worry about and that everyone involved has good intentions. "We do not wish to promote premature death as a solution to all medical suffering," Justice Minister Jody Wilson-Raybould declared to the House of Commons in 2016 upon the tabling of the bill that would legalize MAID. She assured her fellow Parliamentarians that Canada would not be offering assisted death to anyone "with a major physical disability who is otherwise in good health or a person who solely suffers from mental illness."

Wilson-Raybould's Department of Justice was even more explicit in outlining why assisted suicide could only ever be an option for the terminally ill.[39] "To permit it in circumstances where a person is not approaching a natural death could be seen as undermining suicide prevention initiatives and normalizing death as a solution to many forms of suffering" read a backgrounder on the new law.

But perhaps Canada's most glaring missing safeguard is that it doesn't see assisted suicide as a last resort. The Health Canada rules explicitly state that MAID is still an option even in cases where the "unbearable physical or mental suffering" of the patient could feasibly be treated. If a disease can be cured, but under conditions that the patient doesn't "consider acceptable," they can request death instead.[40]

"Getting euthanasia from your doctor is on par with getting pain medications for your pain or surgery for your appendicitis—except you get to decide when you want it, and when you qualify," said Kim, noting that Canada has normalized elective death in scenarios where, say, an elective amputation would still be scandalous.

"No doctor is required to amputate a foot just because a patient prefers not to cure their foot infection with antibiotics,"

2 | Outdoing the Americans at Identity Politics

Here's how Canada became the first country in world history to declare itself guilty of committing an ongoing genocide—a concise representation of just how quickly Canada lost its mind on the issue of identity politics.

It's a rare thing for any country to cop to genocide, but after delivering remarks at a 2019 women's conference in Vancouver, Canadian Prime Minister Justin Trudeau admitted that he was the political leader of a nation-state engaged in the forced extermination of entire people.[1]

Trudeau had just been handed the final report of the National Inquiry into Missing and Murdered Indigenous Women and Girls, a probe he had authorized three years previously. The $100 million inquiry had been struck to investigate outsized rates of homicide committed against Canadian Indigenous women, and recommend "concrete actions" to prevent it. The primary takeaway from the final report was that all of the murders were the fault of a "race-based genocide" being perpetrated by the Government of Canada.

The government's failings were not limited to the high murder rate. Higher rates of Indigenous heart disease and high rates of suicide attempts were deemed the expected result of the Canadian state apparatus pursuing Indigenous policies that were "explicitly genocidal and, even, ongoing."

The use of the word "genocide" didn't sit well with such Canadian figures as Romeo Dallaire, the retired general who had been on the ground at the mass murder of 800,000 civilians during the 1994 Rwandan Genocide.[2] But Trudeau accepted the inquiry's conclusions without reservation, even if it meant that he was accepting responsibility for an "ongoing" genocide.

"Earlier this morning, the national inquiry formally presented their final report in which they found that the tragic violence that Indigenous women and girls experienced amounts to genocide," he said. Trudeau then paused for nine seconds to accommodate cheers and applause from the assembled women's conference.[3]

"Ongoing genocide" immediately became an accepted term of Canadian political discourse. One NDP MP, Leah Gazan has employed the term more than forty times in the Canadian House of Commons.

This was the second time in ten years that the Government of Canada had admitted to a form of genocide. The first was under radically different circumstances. In 2015, one of the first acts of the newly elected Trudeau government was to formally accept the final report of its Truth and Reconciliation Commission. The six-volume report was the result of a seven-year-long official inquiry into the Indian Residential School system, a decades-long program of state-run boarding schools intended to forcibly assimilate Indigenous children into white society.

The report stands as a model of meticulous scholarship. The authors cited troves of archival documents to detail how the system started, who it employed, and where it operated. The commission held cross-country public hearings that interviewed hundreds of former students, many of whom had never previously gone on record with accounts of childhood sexual abuse.

On the delicate subject of children who had died at residential schools, researchers chased down every verifiable death notice they could and sorted the resultant 3,200 names into a public database detailing who had died at which school, and when. An eighty-three-page addendum to the final report included charts plotting known student deaths by year, by region, and by cause (most of them were due to tuberculosis).[4] It included detailed maps showing the abandoned and unmarked cemeteries where they were likely buried. The report also included statistical data to show that even in an era where child mortality was common, the death rate in residential schools was always far higher than the Canadian average.

The Truth and Reconciliation Commission was extremely measured in how it employed the g-word. Obviously, the residential school system had not been a program of organized mass murder; it wasn't a crime on par with the likes of the Rwandan genocide or the Holocaust. But the report did conclude that the residential school system was tantamount to a "cultural genocide," something it defined as "a systematic, government-sponsored attempt to destroy Aboriginal cultures and languages and to assimilate Aboriginal peoples so that they no longer existed as distinct peoples."[5]

The Truth and Reconciliation Commission had the receipts for this. Any number of official documents from the time made clear that the entire point of residential schools was to produce a generation of Indigenous children entirely alienated from the language and traditions of their parents. This was neatly summed up in a 1920 quote from Duncan Campbell Scott, the civil servant in charge of the residential school system at its height. "Our objective is to continue until there is not a single Indian in Canada that has not been absorbed into the body politic and there is no Indian question, and no Indian Department," Scott said in testimony to the Canadian Senate.

The Missing and Murdered Indigenous Women (MMIW) inquiry was a different thing entirely. From the beginning, the process was dominated by veteran political activists. The report's introduction quotes heavily from Pamela Palmater, a Toronto academic who was a founding spokesperson of Idle No More, a left-wing protest movement that has spearheaded efforts to cancel Canada Day and shut down the Canadian oil sector, among other campaigns.

The inquiry was also dealing with a problem much more complex than originally pitched. Indigenous women were indeed being killed at way higher rates than almost anyone else (about five to six times higher than the average). But in almost all of these cases, the killer was also Indigenous. According to a Statistics Canada analysis completed after the MMIW report, 490 Indigenous women were the victims of homicide between 2009 and 2021. "In most cases, the person accused of their homicide was also Indigenous (86%)," it read.[6]

But this statistic is only mentioned in passing in the MMIW report. The report's authors call it "unreliable" without providing contrary evidence; they dismiss the data as "encouraging racism."

In fact, the MMIW report has almost no evidence of any kind. Across more than 1,000 pages, there isn't a single line of criminological analysis of who is getting murdered, under what circumstances, where, and by whom. An addendum simply states "there is no reliable estimate of the numbers of missing and murdered Indigenous women, girls, and 2SLGBTQQIA people in Canada."[7]

Instead, the report spends an inordinate amount of time redefining genocide until it applies to Canada. The addendum argues that prior definitions of genocide, such as the UN definition drawn up in the immediate wake of the Holocaust, failed to consider the act "through a gendered lens." The Truth and Reconciliation Commission was mistaken in suggesting that cultural genocide is any different from actual genocide. And the addendum notes that while Indigenous communities are actually growing faster than almost any other Canadian demographic, this fact "should not discount" the charge of genocide. "In actuality, genocide encompasses a variety of both lethal and non-lethal acts, including acts of 'slow death,'" it wrote.

As to how the Government of Canada could hope to stop committing genocide, the MMIW's "calls for justice" recommends a full course of "decolonization," including the incorporation of "gender-inclusive" language into government forms and "a guaranteed annual livable income for all Canadians, including Indigenous Peoples." An "absolute paradigm shift is required to dismantle colonialism within Canadian society," it read.

The Truth and Reconciliation report had been plainly written by its authors, who wanted a document that could be easily read and understood by the Canadian public. To this day, Indigenous leaders will often say that if Canadians want to understand why residential schools occupy such a calamitous place in native memory, they need to only read the TRC final report. The MMIW report, by contrast, is a thicket of academic jargon. The word "systemic" appears 109 times in the main report. "Patriarchy" appears ten times. "Lived experience" appears forty-seven times. "Colonial" and its variants appear 379 times.

Although the inquiry had been struck to figure out why so many Indigenous women were being abducted and murdered, organizers soon pushed for it to encompass gays, bisexuals, transgender individuals, and every other conceivable non-heterosexual identity. At no point does the report specify how many murdered Indigenous women were gay or transgender, but it did insist on following up every mention of the term "women and girls" with the acronym 2SLGBTQQIA (two-spirit, lesbian, gay, bisexual, transgender, queer, questioning, intersex and asexual).

The tale of the two inquiries would prove a stark illustration of just how quickly Canada had descended into fantasy when it came to discussing its iniquity. As recently as 2015, a Crown inquiry given the sensitive task of probing one of Canada's darkest chapters could return with a stark airing of facts that now stands as the authoritative account of the whole period. Only a few years later, a team given the much simpler task of figuring out how to keep Indigenous women from being murdered could do little more than spit out baseless academic theories about "cultural violence" and "intersectional systems of oppression."

Perhaps unsurprisingly, the MMIW inquiry did nothing to address the very crisis it had been tasked to solve. In 2019, the year that the final report of the MMIW inquiry was made public, forty-eight Indigenous women were victims of homicide. Four years later, the problem was actually a little bit worse; fifty Indigenous women were murdered in 2023.[8]

* * *

Indigenous relations are far from the only corner of Canadian civic life that is now heavily defined by identity politics. Go into the Government of Canada archives, and it's possible to find traces of a time when the official stance on race relations was simply to treat everyone equally. Since the 1980s, Canada's Department of Immigration has completed an annual report on the state of Canadian multiculturalism. Its 2008 edition was entitled "Promoting Integration," and the basic gist was that as Canada got more ethnically heterogeneous as a result of immigration, it was the government's job to ensure that newcomers were offered "economic, social and cultural integration."[9]

Fast-forward to 2021 and Canadian bureaucrats are now attending training sessions in which they are told that treating all races the same ("colorblindness") is actually white supremacist.

Also in the white supremacy category are "Thanksgiving," "meritocracy," "individualism," "perfectionism," and "digital blackface," a term for when white people use an internet meme that features a black person. And if attendees have any quarrel with these claims, that constitutes a "denial of white privilege," another marker of white supremacy.

"Racism is real and this reality will not be questioned," reads an introductory title card.

That all comes from the official 2021 "anti-racism" training materials used by Global Affairs, the federal department in charge of Canadian foreign relations.[10]

Canada's 12,000 or so foreign policy bureaucrats are told that they serve a deeply racist country, even if it doesn't actually have any racist laws or policies on the books. They're told that it's impossible to be racist against white people, since white people are the beneficiaries of Canada's "Eurocentric" system and thus an oppressor class.

The story is similar in the Canadian military. The Canadian Armed Forces are now openly telling service members that they are charged with defending a deeply racist country steeped in oppressive colonialism. "Racism in Canada is not a glitch in the system; it is the system," reads the Department of Defence in its Final Report on Systemic Racism and Discrimination, first published in 2022.[11]

The report says that the entire armed forces are "hampered by the powerful constraints of its inherited colonialist culture." As examples, they cite the Christmas holidays, the presence of "Euro-Canadian" meals in mess halls, or the simple fact that many of them speak French, a language that employs gendered nouns.

Against all this, the military's top leadership pledges itself to "dismantle Canada's colonial culture."

In fact, almost every Canadian institution has an "anti-racism strategy" these days. There's even a Federal Anti-Racism Secretariat charged with pushing Canada into its new "equitable" future. When federal ministers received their mandate letters in the wake of Canada's 2021 federal election, they were all told that they sat atop structures awash in "profound systemic inequities."[12]

The Canadian Association of Chiefs of Police has published anti-racism training materials replete with declarations that Canadian law enforcement serves an oppressive system. "Systemic racism is a well-established concept rooted in our colonial past, embedded in our legislation, enabled in our institutional practices and sustained in our organizational culture," Ottawa Police Chief Peter Sloly is quoted as saying in one anti-racist slide presentation.[13]

The police chiefs even distributed a thirty-seven-page glossary of inclusive terms, including "white fragility," a common charge levelled against white people who challenge the tenets of anti-racism. "White fragility presents in defensiveness or 'defensive moves' such as arguing, silence, or leaving the situation," it reads.[14]

The Canadian "point-based" immigration system has long been considered a model of racial equality, since it was one of the world's first to select only on merit without reference to an immigrant's country of origin. It's one of the singular reasons that Canada is now one of the most ethnically diverse countries on earth. But you wouldn't know it from the anti-racism strategy published by Immigration, Refugees and Citizenship Canada. They declare that Canada is a society that elevates "white people (or settler groups) above everyone else in many areas of Canadian life. The inertia continues to be upheld by access, privilege, and indifference."

Public school teachers in Toronto are now supplied with "challenging oppression" guides telling them to become agents of "decolonization" and to always consider the "identity group" of any student they talk to. "Race matters—it is a visible and dominant identity factor in determining people's social, political, economic, and cultural experiences," reads an introduction.[15]

The same pamphlet declares that the very act of education is "a colonial structure that centers whiteness." It goes on: "Therefore it must be actively decolonized."

The name for all this is "critical race theory" (CRT). Developed in the United States, the doctrine holds that the entire institutional structure of the West is fundamentally racist and that the only solution is special treatment for what the Canadian government now officially refers to as "equity-deserving groups."

Or, as the Canadian Armed Force's official "anti-racism lexicon" puts it, CRT is the idea "that race is a social construct, and that racism is not merely the product of individual bias or prejudice, but also something embedded in legal systems and structures and perpetuates racial inequities."[16]

The most pernicious part of CRT is that it doesn't require overt discrimination. Even if every single prejudicial law or regulation is done away with, any material difference in outcomes between ethnic groups is evidence enough of a "systemic racism" continuing to infect the system.

If the ethnic proportions of the prison population do not match those groups' shares of the wider population, it's because of a racist judicial system. If universities are accepting some races more than others, it's because of racist eligibility requirements.

Canadian race relations used to prioritize equality of opportunity. But after Canada's wholesale embrace of CRT, the goal is now "equity," defined as equality of outcome.

Whereas equality requires Canadians to ignore each other's immutable characteristics, equity requires the exact opposite: a constant obsession with the various "intersecting" identities of one's fellow citizens and the design of policies to accommodate them.

"Throughout Canada's history, the existence of systemic and cultural racism has been enshrined in regulations, norms, and standard practices," reads the Department of Defence's Final Report on Systemic Racism and Discrimination.[17]

The same document contends that if the share of women and "racialized people" in the military isn't exactly representative of the wider population, it's due solely to "archaic paradigms and systemic barriers" that prevent these groups "from naturally thriving in the workplace."

The solution, writes Canada's defense chiefs, is "artificially increasing the representation of women, Indigenous, Black and other racialized people, and people with disabilities" until these "archaic paradigms" can be rooted out and destroyed.

CRT was designed with the United States in mind, and as it's been imported into Canada and embraced at the highest levels, there's often been little to no effort to tailor its nostrums to the Canadian landscape.

Global Affairs' anti-racism training materials cite heavily from US literature and explain this away by saying that the United States and Canada are exactly the same when it comes to race relations. "Truth be told, racism is just as bad in Canada," it states.

One huge oversight in this claim is that Canada has no significant legacy of slavery. There was indeed African slavery in the British colonies that would form Canada, but it had been illegal for more than forty years upon Canada's 1867 founding as an independent country, and it had been nowhere near as widespread or economically important as slavery to the South.

In the United States, virtually anyone with African heritage is only a few generations away from an ancestor who lived in bondage on US soil. In Canada, it's the reverse. Only about 4,000 people total were held as Canadian slaves across the 200 years preceding abolition.[18] As a result, Canada's 1.5 million black citizens are descended almost entirely from African and Caribbean immigrants who have come to Canada since the 1970s.

Regardless, slavery factors heavily into official Canadian anti-racism documents. The country's official Anti-Racism Strategy defines anti-Black racism as being rooted in "enslavement," and says that it is "deeply entrenched in Canadian institutions, policies and practices." So much so, that "anti-Black racism is either functionally normalized or rendered invisible to the larger white society."[19]

It's in keeping with a Canadian anti-racism movement that never seemed to be particularly concerned about whether it was addressing a problem that actually existed.

One of Canada's many anti-racism initiatives has been a program to start categorizing national statistics by ethnicity. The idea being to provide regular updates on the extent of Canada's "systemic racism" problem.

In a 2023 report for the Calgary-based Aristotle Foundation, financial analyst Matthew Lau parsed through all these new numbers and uncovered results that were not in keeping with a country that was supposedly awash in white privilege and systematized racism. When it came to weekly earnings, white Canadians were in the middle of the pack when ranked against the other races. Among women, white people didn't even make the top five; workers of Korean, Chinese, South Asian, Japanese, Filipino, and Arab heritage were all earning more money.

It was similar when it came to test scores, university enrolment, and representation in elite professions such as medicine or engineering: Canadians with Asian or Middle Eastern background were all doing noticeably better than their white counterparts.

Indigenous and Black Canadians did indeed lag on every indicator. But Lau's argument was that if Canada was truly a bastion of institutionalist white supremacy, you would at least expect white people to be on the podium when it came to earnings or educational attainment. "The evidence to support the claim that Canada is rigged to disfavour racial minorities is indeed scant—at best," he wrote.[20]

If anti-racism theory and practice have been particularly able to thrive in Canada, it might be because the idea of treating Canadians differently based on their race is actually encoded in the Constitution. The Charter of

Rights and Freedoms, which entered into force in 1982, states that "every individual is equal before and under the law ... without discrimination." But it immediately follows this up with a caveat stating that it precludes "any law, program or activity that has as its object the amelioration of conditions of disadvantaged individuals." This is the "affirmative action" clause, and it effectively declares that discrimination is legal, provided the beneficiary is "disadvantaged."

At the time of the Constitution's passage, affirmative action was largely confined to programs designed to encourage women into managerial positions. Canada had a federally run "affirmative action directorate" at the time, but its job mostly involved pitching woman-friendly training policies to the private sector. Quotas were a no-no, as was any policy that risked elevating unqualified candidates. "When you put a woman in a position when she's not qualified or interested, you're setting up a situation where there's a good chance of failure," Marg Guillet, an affirmative action officer for the Windsor School Board, told the *Windsor Star* in 1982.[21] She added, "from that failure, you've done harm to the education system."

But as soon as anti-racism had instilled itself in Canada's upper echelons, the affirmative action clause meant that there was an endless runway to go all-out on a system of race-segregated jobs, grants, and government programs.

In the United States, these kinds of actions risk bumping up against anti-discrimination lawsuits. In Canada, the Charter of Rights and Freedoms explicitly declares that it's not real discrimination.

Probably the most noticeable example has come in the form of job postings that routinely specify the preferred racial characteristics of the applicant. As recently as 2013, it became a miniature scandal when a casting agency connected with the Canadian Broadcasting Corporation advertised for a children's show host that was "any race except Caucasian."[22] As soon as the ad circulated on social media, it was pulled down. CBC and the casting agency issued public apologies. We made a mistake and we're apologizing profusely. I'm mortified," casting contractor Larissa Mair told the *National Post*.

Less than ten years later, it is the rare government posting that *doesn't* mention race. When Transport Canada hires aviation safety inspectors, it now specifies that priority will be given to applicants from "equity-deserving groups."[23]

In one June 2024 hiring push, the Department of National Defence posted twenty jobs, eighteen of which contained disclaimers that hiring would be prioritized for "Indigenous peoples, members of visible minorities, people with disabilities, and women."[24]

The Canada Summer Jobs program, which allows nonprofits to apply for summer students whose salaries are paid by the government, now openly favours applicants who pledge to hire "Black and other racialized youth, Indigenous youth, and 2SLGBTQI+ youth."[25]

And the race screening becomes particularly overt when it comes to federal funding of research and academia. The Canadian Institutes of Health Research (CIHR) now hands out research funding using a complex quota system favouring applicants "who self-identify as a racialized person or who self-identify as a person with a disability."[26] The agency ensures that these groups receive funding at exactly the same proportion as their cohort's share of grant applications. In the pre-quota era, the figures were actually pretty close. "Racialized persons" submitted 26 percent of the applications and received 21.9 percent of the grants. But CIHR declares that this isn't good enough and infers that the 3.1 percent gap is evidence of "barriers within the health research funding system."

The Government of Canada spends more than $300 million per year on Canada Research Chairs, dedicated research positions across forty-seven Canadian institutions. And increasingly, you can't get one of these positions unless you're racialized or of atypical sexuality. "This call is open only to qualified individuals who self-identify as members of a racial community," read one University of Waterloo posting for a Canada Research Chair in Computer Science.[27]

By federal order, 22 percent of Canada Research Chairs must be visible minorities, 4.9 percent must be Indigenous, and 7.5 percent must have a disability. If those quotas aren't met organically, universities have to start explicitly turning away the able-bodied white people.[28]

And the culture of explicit race segregation has permeated Canadian universities well beyond the areas in which Ottawa retains direct control. Of the 100 MD students admitted each year by Queen's University, ten of the seats are restricted to Black or Indigenous applicants. The ten seats were originally part of an elite program to push gifted students into medical school on an accelerated timeline. But in 2020, this was set aside in favour of a new race-stratified plan to emphasize "anti-colonialism" and "cultural safety."[29]

Toronto Metropolitan University did one better: its medical school now admits only one quarter of its students based on the traditional meritocratic route of grades and qualifications. The other 75 percent are admitted based on what the school calls its "Indigenous, Black, and Equity-Deserving admissions pathways."[30]

Schools are even beginning to demarcate race-specific zones and events on campus. The aforementioned University of Waterloo has swim times at its athletic centre restricted solely to "Black folx." According to the official description of the "Black Folx swim," the idea is to encourage participation from a group whose "relationship with water" is spotty.[31]

In 2024, the University of British Columbia (UBC) announced the opening of its first "identity-affirming space available only for Black undergraduate and graduate students." To enter the Black Student Space, UBC students must first file a written application confirming that they "self-identify as Black."[32]

Patanjali Kambhampati is a chemistry professor at McGill University who specializes in ultrafast laser science. When grant applications started including queries about whether the applicants would be prioritizing diversity and inclusion in their hires, Kambhampati made a point of politely side-stepping them. "We will hire the most qualified people based upon their skills and mutual interests," he wrote on two applications that were swiftly rejected, one of them citing the fact that "the Equity, Diversity and Inclusion considerations in the application were deemed insufficient."

For Kambhampati, an Indian immigrant whose grandfather had joined Mohandas Gandhi's struggle against British Imperialism, it seemed as if the Canadian establishment had been taken over by a new religion. "There are now many positions that are simply off limits to straight white men who are not handicapped," he wrote in a 2022 op-ed.[33] "One must pledge allegiance to these illiberal principles in order to be a practising scientist."

* * *

It was a one-paragraph Facebook post that would forever change Chanel Pfahl's career as an Ontario high school teacher. The forum was a teachers-only Facebook group, and Pfahl was reacting to a colleague encouraging fellow teachers to circulate literature by the group Black Lives Matter, a US activist group whose goals at the time included defunding the police and disrupting the "Western-prescribed nuclear family structure."[34]

"Kids aren't in school to be indoctrinated with CRT. Schools should be nonpartisan. Focus on modelling kindness to everyone and speak out against any form of discrimination you see," wrote Pfahl, before quickly deleting it as outraged replies from other teachers began to pile up.

Still, the damage had been done. One of the teachers in the forum reported Pfahl to her school board, prompting her to be pulled out of class mid-lesson, replaced with a substitute and put in touch with district administrators.

"I got on this Zoom call and they told me that I was going to be suspended for a week without pay. I could not come onto school property, could not speak to parents I had already arranged to speak to that evening, so I just ghosted them," she said. On top of the suspension, Pfahl was also investigated by the Ontario College of Teachers, who after eleven months issued her with an "oral caution."[35]

Throughout her odyssey, Pfahl has maintained social media accounts documenting the sheer tonnage of CRT and other woke causes finding their way into the Canadian public school system:

- A display about "white woman tears" on an Ontario school bulletin board read: "White women use their tears to advance themselves at the expense of people of colour."
- Worksheets at a Mississauga elementary school asked students to write down the skin colours of themselves, their family, and their friends. A list of suggested colours includes "wheatish," "peach," and either "light brown" or "dark brown."
- An elementary class in Ontario's Simcoe County instructs eleven- and twelve-year-old students to draw up "identity wheels" detailing their race, ethnic background, gender identity, and sexual orientation. "Pansexual" wrote one. "Non-binary" wrote another.
- A grade-three class in Ontario's Peel District School Board asked students to describe "privilege." "Privlege means when something is easier like white people have more privlege than black," read the crooked handwriting of one child's submission.
- A grade-nine science project in Brampton asked students to profile famous fictional scientists, except that the only details they were asked to include were the scientists' race, sex, economic class, mother tongue, and sexual orientation.
- An assembly at a Surrey, BC elementary school convened to teach about the ubiquity of "systemic racism," while a Surrey high school mounted an "anti-capitalist Christmas" display in its halls: "You are a worker and a consumer trying to be in false class solidarity with billionaires," it read.

Pfahl isn't getting these reports from fellow dissidents. All she has to do is grab them off the publicly available Facebook and X.com accounts of schools and teachers.

And it's not just the classroom. Even a meeting with the mental health nurse can veer into a discussion of anti-racism. School Mental Health Ontario is an arm of the Ontario government tasked with providing early intervention for mental illness in the public school system. In 2020, the group published materials asserting that racism was a "socially-contracted mental illness" that many white people weren't even aware they had. "Anti-Black racism is deeply entrenched in Canadian institutions, policies and practices, to the extent that it is either functionally normalized or rendered invisible to the larger White society," read the info sheet.[36] As examples of this "covert racism," the pamphlet cited the existence of "English-only" school materials or even just a white student uttering the line "my intention was not racist."

Pfahl says that all of this activism has only ever been pushed by a vocal minority of teachers and administrators; she suspects it's between 5 and 10 percent. But as was illustrated in her case, the vocal minority has immense scope to punish or harass anyone who doesn't follow the party line.

The totemic case of this was Richard Bilkszto, a Toronto school principal who in 2021 was forced to attend an anti-racism training session in which a trainer singled him out as an icon of white supremacy.

According to a statement of claim later filed by Bilkszto, he said he pushed back against an assertion by session leader Kike Ojo-Thompson that racism in Canada was just as bad as in the United States. "We are here to talk about anti-Black racism, but you in your whiteness think that you can tell me what's really going on for Black people?" he was told in reply, with Ojo-Thompson citing the comment in future sessions as an example of being "accosted by white supremacy."

A review by the Workplace Safety and Insurance Board would later agree with Bilkszto's assertion that he had been subject to "workplace harassment and bullying." But the principal, who had spent most of the interim months with deep depression, would take his own life in July 2023 soon after launching a formal lawsuit against the Toronto District School Board.[37]

Some education departments have been more explicit than others in warning staff that adherence to the new norm is not voluntary. In 2023, BC Education Minister Rachna Singh opened Pride Month by sending a letter to parents and teachers, reminding them that celebrations of Pride Month were compulsory across all K-12 classrooms. "All schools must comply with the Human Rights Code and demonstrate they are creating safe, welcoming and inclusive environments for our students and staff," wrote Singh, adding a suggestion that teachers employ "math problems that use 'they/them' pronouns."[38]

Said Pfahl, "I think it's causing a generation of kids that are depressed and anxious; all they're told about their society is that it's systemically oppressive, that they have privileges that they didn't earn."

"Imagine being a child who has all this pressure to be in a group and be accepted and all that. What are you supposed to do?"

3 | The Real Estate Bubble that Never Ever Bursts

When Canadian Mattea Roach logged one of the greatest-ever runs on the game show *Jeopardy!*, one of the first thoughts that struck the Nova Scotia-born contestant was that home ownership was no longer an unobtainable pipe dream. "On some level, it's a little bit grim that I had to go on a game show—and not just appear on a game show but be one of literally the top contestants to ever be on that show—to feel like I have now some chance at like having financial security in my twenties," Roach told the *Toronto Star* in 2022.[1]

And none of what Roach was saying was hyperbole. At the time of the interview, Roach lived in Toronto, where the average home price had just topped $1.25 million.[2] That figure was an average across all home types, including condos and townhouses. For a detached home, the average sale price had exploded to $1.9 million.

Roach would end up walking away from *Jeopardy!* with total winnings of US$560,983. Without accounting for taxes, this was equal to about $730,000 Canadian. It meant that Roach, the sixth-ranked *Jeopardy!* player of all time, would still need to secure a mortgage of at least one million dollars to have any chance at even an entry-level Toronto house. The *Jeopardy!* winnings weren't even enough to buy a condo without financing; those were averaging $821,000 in early 2022.

One of the signature economic trends of this century has been housing prices unmoored from the public's ability to afford them. Across basically the entire English-speaking world, the last twenty years have ushered in a new era in which the prospect of owning a home on a middle income died. But nowhere has this been truer than in Canada. It is Canada that pioneered the idea of seeing whole cities transform into over-leveraged financial products. It is Canada where the problem of unaffordability first began to veer into the cartoonish.

Of late, housing affordability has even started to factor into Canada's internal security planning. In early 2024, Canadian legal scholar Matt Malone obtained a heavily redacted report by the Royal Canadian Mounted Police warning that the populace may start to revolt once they realized their grim economic standing.[3] "The coming period of recession will … accelerate the decline in living standards that the younger generations have already witnessed compared to earlier generations," reads the nine-page document, intended only for discreet circulation within the Canadian federal government. It added that "many Canadians under 35 are unlikely ever to be able to buy a place to live."

And this has all happened with remarkable speed. Imagine if Mattea Roach had scored a record-breaking *Jeopardy!* streak in 2002. Adjusting for inflation, $730,000 would have been equivalent to about $479,190 then. In the Toronto real estate market of 2002, $480,000 would have unlocked a sprawling buffet of housing options for the young *Jeopardy!* champion.

A quick review of real estate listings published in the *Toronto Star* during the fall of 2002 reveals everything from historic houses, luxury lofts, and four-storey townhomes to five-bedroom McMansions. With a savvy realtor, Roach would have had just enough *Jeopardy!* cash to settle down in an ivy-covered three-bedroom estate in Forest Hill, one of the city's wealthiest neighbourhoods. That property, 159 Eastbourne, was listed for $499,900 in October 2002.[4] Now, it's in a neighbourhood where the starting price is north of $1.5 million.

If *Jeopardy!* champions can barely afford a place to live, what of everybody else? While the unaffordability crisis was once the sole preserve of major centres such as Vancouver and Toronto, it has now spilled out even into the country's secondary markets. In 2023, the Royal Bank of Canada calculated that even in traditionally affordable cities like Edmonton or Calgary, more than half of families were too poor to qualify for the mortgage on an average home.[5]

The Atlantic province of New Brunswick used to be renowned as a far-flung kingdom of cheap houses. It was the place where private islands or sprawling estates could literally be had for the same price as a Vancouver condo. This was because New Brunswick had a stagnant economy and a shrinking population. It still has both of those things, but nobody can afford a mortgage. In just four years between 2019 and 2023, New Brunswick home prices soared by an incredible 68 percent.[6]

In 2013, an average New Brunswick home went for $159,267. Ten years later, the average was $297,527. This works out to an increase of about $260 per week. To put it another way, for every month that a young New Brunswicker saved up for a down payment on their first home, the price of that home went up by more than $1,000.

Compounding everything is the simple fact that Canada, of all places, should have the means to build as many homes as it wants. The country does not lack land; it's one of the world's most sparsely populated countries, ranking just below Iceland and Botswana. It you divide Canada's entire land mass by its population, every man, woman and child would have more than six hectares (15 acres) each. That's just enough land for every Canadian to build their own private Parliament Hill.

Even if you omit all the land that's permanently frozen, there's still enough Canada for everyone to have space for a couple dozen private hockey rinks. And there's certainly no shortage of building materials. It takes between twenty and fifty trees to build an average-sized residential house. Canada has approximately 318 billion trees.[7]

Canada's natural endowments explain why, historically, housing crunches have represented only brief inconveniences to its economy. When the post-war Baby Boom gave way to rising rent and home prices in the late 1960s, the federal government simply began handing out tax credits and interest-free loans until whole cities were being carved out of the wilderness each year.

At the height of the homebuilding spree in 1974, there was a new home built for every 100 Canadians. Compare that to 2022, when builders churned out just 219,942 homes, or about one for every 177 Canadians.[8]

By the late 1980s, Canada had been so packed with subdivisions and new condos that federal housing minister Stewart McInnes proudly declared, "Canadians are now among the best-housed people in the world."[9]

It only took a generation for the opposite to become true. For three consecutive years (2016 to 2018), the OECD charted the Canadian real estate market as having the worst "price to income" ratios in the developed world.[10] And as of 2024, Canada remains second only to Portugal in the ranking.

So, as Canada finds itself at the sharp end of the new world in which attainable home ownership is going extinct, its citizens have the unique humiliation of knowing that their crisis is almost entirely manufactured.

* * *

The cause of the Canadian unaffordability crisis is simple: there are not enough homes to go around. As of the 2021 census, Canada had 16,284,235 private dwellings and 36,991,981 people. Or, about one dwelling for every 2.3 people. That's a homes-to-person ratio lower than any other country in the G7.[11]

And the Canadian "housing gap" keeps getting progressively worse. For at least the past two decades, the rate of Canadian homebuilding has not come close to keeping pace with the rate of population growth. With each passing year, there are more Canadians sharing fewer homes.

In 2023, the Canadian Mortgage and Housing Corporation set out to calculate just how bad this housing shortage had gotten. They estimated that Canada had fallen behind by an incredible 3.5 million homes and that real estate wouldn't again become affordable until that gap could somehow be patched up.[12]

To get an idea of just how many homes that is, imagine that Canada just started seizing US territory until it had enough extra houses to plug the gap. Canada would have to conquer the border states of Vermont (334,000 total homes), Montana (515,000 total homes), Idaho (752,000 total homes), New Hampshire (639,000 total homes), Maine (739,000 total homes), and Alaska (326,000 total homes) to make up the difference.[13] Or to use a Canadian example, the country would need to build at least two Alberta's worth of extra homes. Alberta is the country's fourth-largest province. As of the 2021 census, it had 1.6 million occupied private dwellings.

How this happened is where the issue gets a bit more complicated. There's no singular reason why Canada neglected to build two Albertas worth of houses. It's what happens when a country spends twenty to thirty years deciding that almost everything is more important than homebuilding.

Canadian municipal governments have been almost cartoonishly anti-densification. Most Canadian cities have long made it illegal to build anything but a single-family home on most residentially zoned land.

In Vancouver, about 80 percent of the city is zoned for single-family detached homes.[14] In Toronto, it's about 62 percent.[15] In Calgary, it's 67 percent.[16] And getting any of those low-density lots up-zoned is to enter a Kafkaesque nightmare of endless red tape and public roundtables about "neighbourhood character."

This is something a coalition of Vancouver-area First Nations encountered firsthand when they proposed to develop a patch of Indigenous-owned land into a forest of condo towers housing up to 24,000 people.

Neighbours greeted the project with an all-out campaign to get the plans scrapped in favour of something smaller. At one extended Vancouver City Council meeting, multiple petitioners told the Indigenous developers that the high-density project didn't seem all that "Indigenous." "I was born and raised in Vancouver on this stolen land by British colonizers," said one opponent, before adding that the developer's Coast Salish Indigenous ancestors would be ashamed of "this monstrous development on these sacred lands."[17]

Environmental policies have both limited the amount of land on which to build and have vastly increased the complexity and cost of building. The most famous example of a Canadian government actively closing off land to housing development was in 2005 when Ontario drew up a massive "greenbelt" around the so-called Golden Horseshoe, a string of cities bordering Lake Ontario that comprise about one-quarter of the Canadian population.

The idea was to limit urban sprawl, but the whole plan was agnostic as to where all the homebuilding should go if not the borderlands. It didn't go anywhere; it just plunged the region into shortage. A 2018 analysis by the C.D. Howe Institute estimated that Greenbelt restrictions had added as much as $100,000 to the cost of a new home.[18]

All the while, the Bank of Canada kept interest rates at historic lows from 2009 straight through to 2022. For thirteen years, debt was cheaper than at any point in the country's history. The benchmark rate never rose above 2 percent and at one point, dropped to a record low of 0.25 percent. Compare this to the much more affordable period from 1975 to 1990, when interest rates never dropped below 5 percent and once peaked as high as 20 percent. The cheap debt of the 2010s radically increased the mortgage size available to the average homebuyer and allowed hundreds of billions in extra financing to pour onto an already overheated real estate market.

And finally, Canadian homes have been made more expensive by the fact that absolutely everything related to them has been buried in taxes and fees. In a 2023 report, the Canadian Home Builder's Association calculated that the average unit in a Vancouver high-rise building racked up $125,542 in development fees before a single shovel was put in the ground.[19] Even when adjusting for inflation, that kind of money could have purchased the entire condo as recently as the 1970s.[20]

The situation isn't much better in cities across Ontario. In the last twenty years, the province's municipalities have raised development costs from between 300 to 2,000 percent.[21] To build anything in the City of Toronto, the fees alone now cost about $52,000 for a studio apartment and $137,000 for a duplex.[22]

The end result of all of this is an entire generation of Canadians who have abandoned all hope that they'll ever be able to afford property on a normal income. In April 2024, pollster Ipsos asked this as bluntly as it could. Survey respondents were asked if "owning a home in Canada is now only for the rich," and 80 percent said "yes." Of those who didn't already own a home, nearly three-quarters (72 percent) also said they had "given up on ever owning a home."[23]

Sealing off home ownership from all but the rich has had a whole cascade of consequences beyond a bunch of angry young people. The Canadian fertility rate is now among the lowest on the planet. As of 2024, just 1.26 children are born per Canadian woman; only Italy, Japan, and South Korea have lower fertility rates.

As recently as 2008, Canada's fertility rate had stood at a respectable 1.7. As to how it's plummeted so quickly, the survey data seems to show that property-stressed couples simply can't afford more than one or two children. A 2023 survey by the Christian think tank Cardus found that 72 percent of Canadian women under thirty would "ideally like more children" and that childbearing, much like housing, was increasingly becoming the domain of the wealthy. "Richer Canadians have more children," they found.[24]

Thanks to constantly rising prices, the Canadian economy is now dangerously concentrated in real estate. In late 2023, Re/Max announced that real estate now represented 40 percent of Canadian GDP—which is way beyond what should be typical in a healthy economy.[25] In the United States, it's only 18 percent.[26]

If a four-bedroom in the Toronto suburbs can double its value every decade, it's hard to convince investors to buy anything that *isn't* a house. The result is that Canada isn't investing in the usual things that increase wages or grow the economy, such as innovation or productivity. Investment capital is simply locked into an endless cycle of bidding up the same properties over and over.

Meanwhile, Canada transforming its entire housing stock into a high-yield, no-risk financial product, has sparked an entire sub-crisis of foreign buyers parking their money in empty homes. In a single six-week period in 2016, 10 percent of all real estate sales in Metro Vancouver was by foreign buyers.[27] That same year, census data found that more than 60,000 homes in the region were counted as not being occupied by "usual residents," a term that generally means it's sitting empty.[28] Naturally, billions of foreign dollars flowing in to bid up housing that nobody lives in has only worsened the affordability problem.

With hindsight, it's possible to date, almost to the month, when Canadian real estate prices first began their dizzying ascent into insanity. In 2021, Macquarie Group economist David Doyle charted more than forty years of data on home prices versus after-tax income. Starting in 1975, he compared how much money it took to buy a home versus how much Canadians had to spend on housing.

For the first twenty-five years, the numbers were basically the same; there were ups and downs in the housing market, but on average, home prices tracked almost perfectly with income. Right around 2003, the "home price" line on Doyle's chart suddenly pulls away from the "income" line, beginning a feverish ascent that only becomes sharper with time.[29]

Normally, when crazy deviations like this start to show up in real estate charts, it's a sign that a "correction" is on the horizon. When steep lines started to hit US real estate charts in the mid-2000s, it turned out to be the harbinger of the 2008 subprime mortgage crisis. In just a few months, one-fifth of US real estate value evaporated.[30]

In Canada, the correction never comes.

It famously didn't come in 2008, when Canada almost entirely avoided the real estate carnage seen in the United States. "In Canada, what happened in 2008/09 reinforced the idea that housing never fails, that a house can only go up," Doyle told the *National Post* in 2021.

It didn't come in 2014, when the Bank of Canada estimated that the housing market was overvalued by as much as 30 percent.[31] In fact, for any Canadian born after 1990, every year of their adult life has been one where the average Canadian home is more expensive than it was the year before.

Policymakers have acknowledged that this is a problem. When a rookie MP named Justin Trudeau first took his seat in the House of Commons in 2008, one of the first things he mentioned was the high cost of Canadian housing. "High housing costs mean young people and new Canadians cannot buy homes, which leads to increased pressure on existing affordable housing," said Trudeau.[32]

But many of the solutions rolled out under the banner of "making housing affordable" have only made the problem worse. At the federal level, one of the first sops to the affordability crisis was a 2015 Conservative promise to allow Canadians to withdraw up to $35,000 from their RRSP to cover a down payment. When a Liberal government took over, it would keep the RRSP plan and eventually raise the withdrawal limit to $60,000. Later, it would introduce a First-Time Home Buyer Incentive, a government loan meant to further increase the amount available to spend on a down payment. These are "demand-side" policies, and all they've done for housing affordability is to free up more money to throw at real estate, thus bidding up prices even further.

But governments keep announcing them because they give politicians something to show to priced-out voters without actually doing anything to bring down real estate prices, which would risk alienating the much larger demographic of voters who own all that inflated real estate. This is something brought up often by UBC Professor Paul Kershaw, who runs the advocacy group Generation Squeeze. "We have long believed there is a cultural addiction to high and rising home prices in Canada, and politicians are leery to disrupt it," Kershaw told the *Vancouver Sun* in 2023.[33]

As of the last count, in 2021, the total value of all of Canada's residential real estate had swelled to $6.1 trillion.[34] That's nearly three times Canada's annual GDP. So even a one percent reduction in prices represents the immediate evaporation of $61 billion in value.

The Canadian weakness for propping up housing demand was put into particularly stark relief in the immediate wake of COVID-19. Throughout the pandemic, the federal government had fire-hosed hundreds of billions of dollars into the Canadian economy. With nowhere else to spend it, Canadians began bidding up real estate even faster than before. Nobody was spared this time around. Even a middle-of-nowhere jurisdiction like Prince Edward County, Ontario (population 24,000) was seeing home prices spike by 78 percent in a single twelve-month period.[35] In Nova Scotia, home prices rose from a pre-pandemic average of $256,103 to $359,225 in just two years.[36]

Even as Canadian civic life returned to normal, the COVID-19 housing bubble didn't burst. The housing market "cooled" and "slowed"—one economist referred to the brief slump as "a reallocation of activity over time."[37] But after just two years, even the most absurd COVID-19-era price gains were locked in as the new norm. By Christmas 2023, the real estate agency Royal Lepage was announcing that in only a few more months home prices would be "back to their pandemic peak."[38]

Helping things along had been yet another package of demand-side policies. The 2022 federal budget introduced the First Home Savings Account, allowing buyers to save $40,000 for a down payment tax-free. It also doubled a First-Time Home Buyers' Tax Credit from $5,000 to $10,000. By 2024, the feds would approve extended amortization terms for mortgages and raise the price cap for insured mortgages from $1 million to $1.5 million.

And then, just for good measure, immigration rates were sent into the stratosphere. Starting in 2022, the Canadian federal government approved record-breaking increases in every conceivable Canadian migration stream. The influx of new permanent residents was hiked to a new target of 465,000 per year starting in 2023, rising to 500,000 by 2025. For context, this is nearly double the 260,000 new immigrants Canada was accepting in 2014, and that was considered high at the time. Statistics Canada had called it "one of the highest levels in more than 100 years."[39]

And in addition to all the new permanent residents, the gates were thrown open virtually for every other immigration stream, from foreign students to temporary foreign workers. Even illegal border crossers were encouraged to pack their bags for Canada. Roxham Road, a popular illegal crossing on the Quebec/New York State border, had been shut down in early 2020 amid a wave of public health lockdowns. But in November 2021, the federal government announced that it was back open for business. Roxham Road would serve as the primary conduit for more than 20,000 additional illegal border crossers until it was eventually closed for good in 2023.[40]

The resulting migration figures are just eyewatering. In 2022 alone, Canada added more than a million people, almost all of it driven by immigration.[41] With population growing by up to 1 percent in a single quarter, it instantly transformed Canada into one of the fastest-growing countries on earth, a distinction it shared exclusively with high birthrate countries in the developing world such as Syria or South Sudan.[42] In the same year that Canada cracked a million newcomers, a near-identical number of immigrants (1,018,000) were accepted into the United States. The United States, with about 340 million people, was far more capable of absorbing them.

Canada's immigration numbers soon became higher even than the early twentieth century, when the country had pursued a deliberate policy of packing as many homesteaders into the Prairies as possible as an assertion of sovereignty in newly occupied (and relatively empty) territory. Of course, housing had been a moot point in the 1910s. If newcomers were wondering where they were going to live, the answer was that they had to build a dwelling out of logs or sod before the arrival of winter.

That was definitively not the case this time around. At the time the immigration spike was greenlit, Canada was only building about 220,000 new homes per year.[43]

Even if every single one of these new homes packed five people into it, the net effect on Canada would have been to break even. Any new housing capacity would have been immediately absorbed by new immigration, and Canada's housing gap of 3.5 million units would remain untouched.

Importantly, most of the 220,000 new homes were condos; fitting any more than two or three people into one of them would have required a futon in the kitchen. So the shortage just got worse.

Shelter costs, and particularly rent, soared like never before. In 2023 alone, the average Canadian renter saw their rent rise by 8.6 percent. And it gets really crazy when looking at "asking rents": the advertised price of a unit being put back onto the market. That rose by more than one-fifth in just two years. At the end of 2023, a standard Canadian apartment was about $400 per month more expensive than it was at the beginning of 2022, according to Rentals.ca.[44]

Government analysts had warned that this was going to happen. And it was never a particularly controversial prediction. Anybody with a basic grasp of arithmetic would have been able to figure out that one million newcomers per year were going to immediately put upward pressure on rents. In 2022, staffers at Immigration, Refugees and Citizenship Canada had compiled an extremely easy-to-understand PowerPoint presentation explaining to their bosses that if too many new people came to Canada, there wouldn't be enough places for them to live. "Policy-makers must understand the misalignment between population growth and housing supply, and how permanent and temporary immigration shapes population growth," read one slide, which was later obtained in an access to information request by the Canadian Press.[45]

Canadian financial analysts were issuing entire reports detailing how none of this was remotely sustainable. "Immigration is excessive, full stop," Bank of Nova Scotia economist Derek Holt told the *Wall Street Journal* in December 2023.[45] In an update to investors at the time, Holt noted that Canada was adding a large city's worth of newcomers every three months. "That's like presto, here's a new city of London, Ontario created in one quarter," he wrote.

And yet, it just kept going. More than 1.2 million arrived in 2023; another 240,955 arrived in just the first three months of 2024.[46]

Throughout 2023, members of the federal cabinet had made a point of visiting as many affordable housing projects as they could. Often clad in hard hats, they would stand behind a lectern labelled "Building More Homes, Faster" and announce that relief was on the way. But at almost every one of these appearances, they were cutting ribbons on projects that would be overwhelmed by only a few hours' worth of new immigrants.

In July 2023, Prime Minister Justin Trudeau made a special trip to Hamilton, Ontario to announce $45 million in federal monies to build 214 rental units.[47] If each of those units ends up housing the average Canadian household size of 2.5, they'll shelter 535 people in total. Canada was adding about 140 people an hour. So, in the time it took Trudeau to fly to Hamilton, make a speech and then fly home, the units were already a moot point.

The reason for the immigration surge was never fully articulated. Canadian cabinet ministers have been asked repeatedly why they allowed immigration to spike well beyond the country's ability to absorb it. And the answer has usually been that immigration drives growth, or that the country had a labor shortage, or simply that Canadians love immigrants.

"We are extremely fortunate that … we have the social capacity to welcome immigrants," said Finance Minister Chrystia Freeland in the wake of the aforementioned report in which her own advisors had warned her that immigration would send affordability into a tailspin.[48]

* * *

Thousands of policy decisions lay along Canada's long road to the world's most unaffordable homes. Propping up every $3.5 million Vancouver teardown or

$1 million Brampton, Ontario bungalow is a latticework of decisions made by everyone from city councillors to central bankers to the prime minister himself.

As this book goes to press, Canadian governments have started to slowly adopt policies that aren't just another package of demand-side incentives. Foreign buyers are now under much tighter restrictions. BC and Ontario have led efforts to steamroll the municipal grip on zoning and to ram through blanket approvals on higher-density housing. In much of BC, starting in 2024, it's now illegal for most cities to zone a lot for anything smaller than a six-plex.

All the while, the federal government is opening underutilized crown land for home construction and punishing antidevelopment cities by withholding federal infrastructure dollars.

But it's telling that when federal lawmakers face the easiest possible test to keep Canadian housing prices within normal boundaries, they failed it in the most spectacular way possible.

In a binary choice between "keep shelter costs stable" or "become one of the fastest growing countries on earth for no apparent reason," the latter option won without a second thought.

4 | Harm Reduction on Crack

In June 2023, BC's chief coroner, Lisa Lapointe, held a dedicated press conference to state that "diversion" was not a problem and that anyone saying otherwise was potentially getting children killed.[1]

Lapointe was a vocal champion of a new BC program of "safer supply." Starting in 2021, BC had began supplying free recreational opioids to the province's drug addicts on the premise that it would steer them away from adulterated black-market drugs.

The way safer supply typically works is that a doctor lines up an addict with a free prescription for a daily supply of opioids, usually hydromorphone or oxycodone. The drugs can then be picked up every day at conventional pharmacies, although in some very specific cases there are programs to deliver the opioids to wherever the user is living, be it a tent encampment or shelter.[2]

Even before the program was launched, there had been concerns that the opioids would be "diverted." It was expected that rather than addicts doing the government drugs, they would flip them for cash and put the proceeds toward black-market drugs, which yielded a better high. When reports began to emerge that this precise scenario had come to pass, Lapointe summoned the press to denounce it for "increasingly polarized rhetoric that is not informed by evidence." She claimed reports of diversion were "clearly not defensible if you look at the data."

The data Lapointe was citing was that government-supplied hydromorphone was not showing up in all that many autopsies of BC overdose victims. It was showing up in some, but not a "significant" number, Lapointe said from a lectern at the BC Parliament buildings.[3] The chief coroner didn't cite any data to disprove claims that diversion was happening, or that flooding all these extra drugs into the system might be swelling the ranks of BC's drug addicts. But Lapointe did insist that critiques of "safer supply" were "divisive," and that divisive language "is the most harmful thing we can do."

Meanwhile, if provincial health authorities had bothered to do a simple Google search, they would have uncovered a province utterly awash in cheap government opioids. Only a few months after the Lapointe press conference,

Postmedia columnist Adam Zivo detailed a spate of posts on the website Reddit advertising "dillies" obtained through safer supply.[4] The term is slang for Dilaudid, a common hydromorphone brand name. And the government provenance of the dillies was easy to track because users were uploading photos of their safer supply prescriptions in order to authenticate that the pills were genuine.

One user by the name of GapParking9650 even spelled out their username using Dilaudid pills. "Dilly heaven. I heart safer supply," read a caption.

Police officers started noticing that their drug busts were turning up huge freezer bags full of prescription hydromorphone. In early 2023, when Mounties in the BC city of Campbell River raided a compound suspected as a centre of the city's illicit drug trade, they found 3,500 pills originally handed out as a safer supply.[5]

Given that safer supply clients are only allowed a maximum of twenty-eight pills per day, this represented at least 1,250 individual incidents of a drug user handing their safer supply ration to a drug dealer in exchange for cash or something harder, like fentanyl.

This phenomenon was visible to anyone who hung around a pharmacy within walking distance of a tent encampment or homeless shelter. That's what the RCMP did outside a Prince George pharmacy in spring 2024. For ten days, undercover officers observed the same fifty-eight-year-old woman being dropped off by taxi first thing in the morning. There, she proceeded to openly swap heroin and fentanyl for anybody exiting the store carrying a bag of "safer supply."

The Prince George RCMP soon announced in a statement that rather than steering drug users away from the black market, they were being "used as a form of currency to purchase more potent, illicit street drugs."[6]

If BC's chief coroner was prepared to casually dismiss all of this, it was on brand for a Canadian overdose strategy that had become eerily comfortable with ignoring inconvenient information.

Back in 2016, when the rate of overdoses was already being called a "crisis," the number of daily Canadian overdose deaths was eight. As this book goes to press, an average of twenty-two Canadians are dying of a drug overdose every single day, a nearly three-fold increase.[7]

It required an awful lot of people standing behind lecterns and saying everything was fine to get that bad.

* * *

The term "harm reduction" was first coined by social workers in the English city of Liverpool in the late 1980s. Its basic premise was to make drug use safer without worrying about encouraging users to ditch the drugs altogether.

"Harm reduction-oriented services do not require a person to stop using substances as a precondition of care and support," reads a primer from the BC Ministry of Health.[8]

The textbook example is to distribute clean hypodermic needles to injection drug users. The user is not dissuaded from using drugs, but it prevents them from contracting bloodborne illnesses as a result of sharing needles. Thus, harm is reduced.

Particularly in BC, Canada has taken this philosophy to its most flamboyant extremes. Patients admitted to BC hospitals are officially allowed to do illicit drugs at their leisure, provided that they still adhere to smoking rules if they're lighting up a meth pipe. A leaked July 2023 memo by Northern Health, one of five BC regional health agencies, chastised workers over reports that nurses were removing drugs and even weapons from hospital patients. "Staff DO NOT remove personal items from the patient's room, even if there is a knife or something considered a weapon under 4 [inches] long," it read.[9] Programs to distribute clean needles have been expanded to include all manner of drug paraphernalia, from single-use crack and meth pipes to snorting kits.

Toronto Public Health now offers two types of pipes (stem or glass bowl), as well as cookers, acidifiers, and tourniquets, all distributed in brightly coloured bags carrying the city's logo.[10]

It became a minor scandal at a BC school district in 2023 when a drug safety presenter ended their presentation by handing out "safer snorting kits." Inside were plastic straws, cards to cut powdered drugs into snortable lines, and well as a booklet filled with snorting tips. "Have condoms and lube with you. You may want to have sex while high," read one.[11]

The kit came via the Canadian AIDS Treatment Information Exchange (CATIE), a nonprofit heavily funded by government that provides bulk shipments of harm reduction materials to anyone who asks. In 2022, a Canadian AIDS Treatment Information Exchange "safer snorting kit" also featured in a viral TikTok video by a York University student joking that the school had just given her a "coke kit."[12]

BC has been experimenting for years with vending machines that hand out drug paraphernalia. In 2014, what is likely the world's first crack pipe vending machine was installed in Vancouver by the Portland Hotel Society, a major contractor for low-barrier shelters and other homelessness services.[13]

In the fall of 2024, it became a scandal when hospitals in three BC cities installed "Care and Connection" boxes at entrances.[14] A cheerful digital display gave users the option of anything from a Naloxone kit to injection supplies to several types of crack pipes. After a Conservative political candidate posted a video of herself using the machine, its use was suspended.

The vast expansion in available supplies has occurred in tandem with programs to acclimatize city dwellers to the increasingly common sight of discarded needles.

A Toronto safe injection site was criticized in 2023 for putting a sign in its window promising a chocolate bar in exchange for a full container of discarded needles.[15]

In Edmonton, the Alberta capital, city hall commissioned a campaign of "see a needle" bus stop ads featuring cartoon needles and urging residents to call 311 whenever they see one. But the "see a needle" service only applied to sharps spotted on public property; everyone else was directed to a step-by-step online guide on how to clean up used drug needles using salad tongs and old milk jugs. "Although it's always important to be careful, there is minimal risk in picking up a used needle," it assures readers.[16]

Starting around 2018, the BC capital of Victoria began experiencing a spate of incidents of residents being accidentally pricked by discarded needles. This included a three-year-old who stabbed herself on a discarded syringe at a downtown Victoria McDonalds.

In response, city playgrounds were given "safely sweep before you play" signs urging parents to clear any sharps or broken glass out of play areas before letting their children use the equipment.[17]

Canadian high schoolers are now being trained as impromptu overdose paramedics. The Advanced Coronary Treatment Foundation, a group that provides free CPR and defibrillator training in Canadian schools, added overdose reversal to its curriculum starting in 2022. "The landscape of emergency response is changing in Canada due to the increase of opioid overdoses and we all have a role to play," announced the group at the time.[18]

The BC government now operates an entire network of former hotels and nursing homes to serve as "low-barrier" shelters where residents are permitted to do illicit drugs within the facility and are supplied with drug paraphernalia. "BC Housing has found abstinence-based facilities create barriers for those using substances and are counterproductive to addressing the problem of homelessness," wrote BC Housing, the province's official housing agency, in a 2020 policy document.[19]

In 2024, it emerged that staff at one of these shelters, the former Tally Ho Hotel in Victoria, were required to wear respirators on shift due to the near-constant presence of drug fumes in the air. "Many of us have wound up in hospital for six, eight, ten hours," one anonymous staffer told CTV.[20]

Other sites have quickly devolved into focal points for drug and weapons trafficking. In 2016, BC spent $11.2 million to purchase a downtown Victoria care home in order to house the evicted residents of a longstanding tent encampment. Overnight, the 147-room facility, now called Johnson Street Community, prompted an explosion of on-street chaos. In just its first few months of operation, Victoria police charted a 256 percent increase in 911 calls related to "public disorder."[21] Soon, police were regularly busting up whole criminal enterprises operating out of the building. In one July 2022 raid, they found two suites loaded with a small arsenal of illegal weapons ranging from shotguns to body armour to axes.[22]

In a 2024 speech to the Greater Victoria Chamber of Commerce, Victoria Police Chief Del Manak said the city's network of low-barrier hotels had been very easily converted into criminal base camps. All criminals had to do was pretend to be someone "experiencing homelessness" and they'd get a free, centrally located suite that they could stuff with drugs and weapons. "They embed themselves in the very facilities where people are vulnerable and marginalized. And then they're able to exploit them," said Manak.[23]

Even BC's public bathrooms came due for a harm reduction makeover. In the spring of 2024, bathrooms at select BC public libraries were retrofitted to become miniature safe consumption sites, complete with sensors to alert staff if a drug user was no longer moving.[24] The BC government also funded the creation of a Safer Bathroom Toolkit to instruct other agencies and businesses how to do likewise.[25]

The materials note that drug users may prefer to shoot up in public bathrooms even if a safe consumption site is nearby, and that this should be encouraged. "Restricting access to bathrooms or implementing measures to discourage substance use in bathrooms does not work," it reads.

Amid all this official normalization of drug use, any attempt to discourage drug use was simultaneously framed as prohibitionist moralizing that would serve only to get people killed. This was neatly summed up in a BC Supreme Court decision, which effectively ruled that drug users had a Constitutional right to shoot up in playgrounds.

Only a few months after BC decriminalized illicit drugs, the province dialed it back ever so slightly with an amendment restricting illicit drug use within fifteen metres of a playground, skate park, or splash park. Now, if someone was smoking meth or shooting heroin on playground equipment, police were instructed to tell the person to move their activity to a slightly less conspicuous place. According to BC Supreme Court Chief Justice Christopher Hinkson, even this most minor sanction against open-air drug use was a violation of the Constitutional right to "life, liberty and security of the person."

Although Hinkson acknowledged that playgrounds turned into shooting galleries was "concerning," he ruled that asking an addict to move would only prompt them to use somewhere where nobody would notice them collapsing from an overdose.

The power of Canada's anti-stigma forces could be seen in a 2022 episode when David Eby, who was then a few weeks from becoming BC premier, proposed a program of involuntary treatment for hardcore drug addicts. Eby was closer to the issue than most: his pre-politics career had been as a lawyer with Pivot Legal Society, an activist group that had been central to shaping Vancouver's permissive drug and homelessness polices. Now, Eby was saying that a chronic drug user couldn't be saved by harm reduction alone. "I fundamentally disagree with the idea that it is respectful of someone's liberty and human rights to release them into the street to die of an overdose," he told Postmedia.[26]

The proposal was met with universal condemnation from the province's galaxy of harm reduction organizations, most notably the Pivot Legal Society. In a report that strenuously referred to the province as "colonial British Columbia," Pivot called the proposal "genocidal." "Forced treatment is part of a broader spectrum of violent, colonial, racist medical treatment that is historically and contemporarily deployed against people who do not conform to white supremacist, settler logic," they wrote.[27]

When Eby assumed the premier's office, he actively walked back the pledge.[28]

"Addiction is about loss of control. It's about continuing to use despite consequences. In British Columbia, they believe that addiction is a lifestyle factor; it's like being vegetarian," said Marshall Smith.

Since 2018, Smith has been the central figure in a push by the neighbouring Government of Alberta to implement a treatment-centred addiction model deliberately designed as a counterweight to the harm reduction model pioneered in BC. It's much harder and more expensive than harm reduction, but the early results show it's working. Alberta's overdose deaths have begun to drop dramatically while BC's keep rising.[29]

Smith also happens to be a former homeless drug addict, where he had a front-row seat on the "Vancouver model" taking shape. He was a young political staffer for the BC Liberal government in the early 2000s and would be among the delegation that flew to Prague in 2003 for the announcement of Vancouver's winning Olympic bid. In 2004, his cocaine problem spiralled into meth addiction and, in his words, he "ended up vanishing into the streets of Vancouver."[30] He would spend three years as a rake-thin street hustler until, on the advice of Vancouver Police, he entered a government-funded addiction treatment program and got clean.

He said recovery is a much harder sell for an addict where there are now whole neighbourhoods constructed around making it easy to do drugs, which he credited to years of BC aligning its addiction policies with the wishes of drug user activists. And that is indeed a thing in BC. The Vancouver Area Network of Drug Users (VANDU) had been quoted in the BC media nearly 1,000 times since its 1997 founding.

Said Smith, "if you are going to have policies that are led by people who use drugs, you're going to get the same thing over and over again; they want free drugs, they want the police to go away and they want a hotel room they can use in."

* * *

Before there were crack pipe vending machines, before there was a charter right to shoot up in playgrounds, and before a single tablet of "safer supply" had been handed out, there was Insite. Located in the heart of Vancouver's Downtown Eastside, this was the world's first "safe consumption" site and the one that would spur all the others.

Insite opened in 2003 as a three-year pilot project funded by Health Canada. At the time, its primary purpose wasn't the prevention of fatal overdoses. Rather, it was intended to curb the high rates of HIV infection among Vancouver's injection drug users. "We are never going to cure drug addiction, but what we can do is help those who have an addiction to stay alive and stay healthy," Larry Campbell, then the Vancouver mayor, announced at a media tour of the new facility.[31]

Before the trial period had even ended, Insite's operators would announce that the experiment had exceeded their wildest expectations. In a flurry of academic papers published by Insite's operators, they wrote that safe injection had prevented fatal overdoses.[32] It had arrested the spread of HIV and Hepatitis C. It had pushed addicts into detox. It had even reduced crime and made the neighbourhood safer. These would become accepted truths of safe consumption as advocates pushed Insite-style facilities across the rest of Canada and then the world.

"The science is in. Insite saves lives," wrote the Vancouver-based HIV researcher Julio Montaner in a 2011 op-ed.[33]

"Insite has science on its side," read a similar column by Thomas Kerr, who led the initial Insite research team, who would end up being one of the key figures in exporting the safe injection model outside Vancouver.[34]

In 2016, Kerr pitched the people of Seattle on a safe injection site by arguing in the *Seattle Times* that "it was found that the opening of Insite did not lead to increases in crime and did not encourage young people to start injecting."[35]

The Supreme Court of Canada also got aboard the "Insite saves lives" bandwagon, using that exact phrase in a 2011 decision that would extend Insite's license and be instrumental in the rapid expansion of safe injection sites across Canada. "Insite saves lives. Its benefits have been proven. There has been no discernable negative impact on the public safety and health objectives of Canada during its eight years of operation," wrote the justices.

Underlying all of these claims, however, was some incredibly patchy data, most with either Kerr or Montaner listed as co-authors.

One of the most frequent assertions about safe consumption sites is that they improve neighbourhoods. This stems from two studies published by the Insite team. The first, a 2006 paper, concludes that "Insite has not contributed to an increase in drug-related crime in surrounding neighbourhoods."[36] This was based on just two years of limited crime data sourced from the neighbourhood immediately surrounding Insite. Researchers looked at the charge rates for drug trafficking, assault, robbery, and vehicle break-ins and found there were "no obvious differences" between the year after Insite's opening and the year before.

The second study was even more narrow in scope. It dispatched a surveyor to walk the ten blocks around Insite for six hours each week, noting every time they saw discarded drug paraphernalia or a drug user shooting up. The surveyor did this for six weeks before Insite's opening and then twelve weeks after, a cumulative 108 hours. These findings were then plugged into mathematical models, which attempted to control for "confounding" factors such as whether it was raining or whether the surveyor had bumped into police on their rounds.[37]

Insite opened on September 22, 2003, just as Vancouver entered its rainy season. Open-air drug use is naturally going to be very different in August than in the cold, wet months that immediately followed Insite's opening. Given the study's extremely limited time frame, the authors applied a logarithm. "The study's authors were able to conclude that the improvement in public order was a result of the presence of Insite," reads a package prepared by Insite's operators.[38]

As for Insite's singular triumph as a place that "saves lives," most of that goes back to a 2011 study published in *The Lancet*.[39] The authors looked at just five years of overdose data for the neighbourhood within 500 metres of the facility's front door. For the two and a half years prior to Insite's opening, there were fifty-five deaths within walking distance of Insite. For the two and a half years after it opened, there were thirty-three. "These programmes should be considered for assessment where injection drug use is prevalent," it concluded.

"A lot of people who work in the field, and a lot of the general population, knew intuitively that something was not right, that these concepts were antithetical to the values of the community," said Alberta's Marshall Smith. So the strategy was to "publish, publish, publish, publish in an attempt to sway public opinion and convince them of something they didn't really believe. It's one of the biggest gaslighting operations I think we've seen in the history of modern medicine."

And just as BC's chief coroner did with reports of "safer supply" diversion, all this patchy data have been freely wielded to slap down harm reduction's critics as being anti-science ideologues. In 2023, Thomas Kerr celebrated Insite's twentieth anniversary with an official statement declaring that science was on their side. "An important reminder as we once again hear anti-science arguments against health services for people who use drugs," he wrote.[40]

That same year, a forty-four-year-old mother of two, Karolina Huebner-Makurat, was hit and killed by a stray bullet as she walked past the South Riverdale Community Health Centre, a Toronto safe injection site. Huebner-Makurat's death came after months of community complaints that the site was a centre of theft, violence, and open-air drug dealing.

Nevertheless, an internal review drawn up in the wake of the tragedy concluded that these were all just "perceived harms."[41]

"The benefits of (consumption treatment services) are evidence-based," it read, before adding that "research has demonstrated … no significant changes in measures of disorder and crime in the vicinity of the site."

Except that the research cited for the "disorder and crime" claim wasn't even based on Canadian data. It came from a 2023 report analysis of New York City crime data collected in the aftermath of that city opening its first overdose prevention centres in 2021. It was a period when New York City crime rates were still in flux as a result of the COVID-19 pandemic, and given that it only covered the area immediately surrounding the new centres, it necessarily involved extremely small sample sizes.

If the operators of Toronto's South Riverdale Community Health Centre had instead cited crime data from their own city, they would have seen that in the same summer that Huebner-Makurat was killed, the neighbourhood immediately surrounding their facility experienced a 60 percent increase in the police-reported assault, and a 900 percent increase in high-priority 911 calls.[42]

The most comprehensive study to date of the North American opioid crisis was assembled by a seventeen-member commission convened by Stanford University and *The Lancet*. In the commission's final report, published in 2022, one of their conclusions is that the Canadian data on its addictions crisis absolutely sucks.

Aside from quarterly Health Canada reports about how many people have died of drug overdoses, the report said Canada doesn't have any idea of how many of its citizens are using heroin or fentanyl, "how many are addicted to these drugs, how much these drugs are bought and sold for, and how users acquire them." Throughout the entire crisis, all health officials have had to work with is death rates and the occasional "self-report surveys." And even the death rates weren't counted properly until 2016.

"Decades into the worst drug epidemic in its history, this situation is scandalous," it read.[43]

* * *

When Lisa Lapointe first took over as BC chief coroner in 2011, Canada was home to precisely one safe consumption site: Insite. If any kind of Canadian harm reduction regime existed, it was limited to a series of small-scale needle exchange programs in major cities. At the time, it was even tricky to get Naloxone, a nasal spray that instantly reverses the effects of overdoses. Although paramedics usually kept the spray on hand, it wouldn't be until 2012 that the BC Centre for Disease Control began mass distributing the medication in portable sunglasses cases.

When Lapointe left office in 2023, she had helped shape the province into the harm reduction capital of the world that it is now. Widespread distribution of safer supply. More than two dozen safe consumption sites, including nine in Vancouver. Billions of dollars in low-barrier shelters. Starting in 2022, the total decriminalization of illicit drugs for personal use.

In the BC of 2011, 293 people died of drug overdoses. In the BC of crack-pipe vending machines and decriminalized fentanyl, 2,511 died of overdoses in 2023.

And even the 2011 mortality rate was obscene when compared to the death rate of 2003 when Insite opened its doors. At the time, an average of sixty-two British Columbians were dying of drug overdoses each year.

As the addiction crisis continued to get worse, the only solution on offer, at least from official channels, was more harm reduction. Even when the evidence of safer supply diversion became too much to ignore, BC would still manage to claim that the cause was a lack of harm reduction.

A December 2023 report by BC's Provincial Health Officer acknowledges that safer supply may indeed be getting opioids into the hands of "non-intended populations" such as teenagers. But this was chalked up mostly to the fact that the safer supply wasn't offering a powerful enough high. "Diversion should be understood as indicating unmet needs for PWUD (people who use drugs)," declares the report, which calls for safer supply to be expanded to include heroin and fentanyl "in a variety of formulations, including smokeable formulations."[44]

The problem with using harm reduction to address an addiction crisis is that even if the strategy works perfectly, the end result is still an entire class of permanent drug users dwelling constantly on the edge of overdose. Low-barrier shelters can keep them from sleeping rough. Safe consumption sites can keep them from sharing needles or fashioning pipes out of broken lightbulbs. Safer supply can reduce the risk of overdose and eliminate the addicts' need to engage in theft or prostitution to obtain their next hit. Naloxone can bring them back from the dead when the hit is too strong. But with each user, it's only a matter of time before one of those safeguards slips, and another fatal overdose is added to the tally.

And even if safe consumption could completely halt overdoses and safer supply could eradicate the need for a black market, you'd still have whole neighbourhoods filled with erratic men and women covered in sores and utterly twisted by opioid abuse. Even pure, government-supplied heroin delivered through clean needles is going to do catastrophic damage to the human brain with regular use.

Harm reduction always has been pitched as a gateway to recovery. An addict would come in off the street. Eventually, they would trust the staff enough to ask for directions to the nearest detox facility.

Vancouver called it the Four Pillars drug strategy when first rolled out in 2001. Harm reduction was supposed to be a co-equal branch of an addiction strategy that also pursued enforcement, treatment, and prevention. Any dollar going into a clean needle program would be matched by a dollar similarly being directed toward a detoxification clinic, a school antidrug program, or a police crackdown on drug dealers. "Each requires the interaction and support of the other three to help this city-wide framework improve public order and public health," declares the strategy's original framework.[45]

That's not how it worked.

Harm reduction became so obsessed with the avoidance of stigma that the mere mention of the other three pillars became incompatible. Safe injection sites didn't become the first point of contact on a drug user's eventual path to sobriety. They became facilities in which it was official policy to treat drug addiction as normal and sustainable. A 2012 academic paper interviewing Insite nurses included accounts of the nurses choking back feelings of horror when helping to inject healthy young women who were smitten with the "exciting and new" lifestyle of the Downtown Eastside and brought in by their pimps for their first hit of heroin. "Even though I want to tell them to 'run out of there!' it's important that I give them a really good experience so that they come back," said one.[46]

At South Riverdale Community Health Centre, the Toronto safe injection site where a mother was randomly shot in 2023, the harm reduction code of silence was so total that managers were told to ignore everything from managers smoking crack to clients openly using the lobby as a stolen goods market. "One staff member regularly paid a client to steal his booze from the local liquor store. When I asked a former supervisor why this was allowed to happen, the response was: 'We don't talk about it. We don't see it,'" a former worker wrote in a 2023 op-ed for the *National Post*.[47]

Health authorities rewrote the language to stamp out any hint of drug addiction being a bad thing. Vancouver's original Four Pillars strategy referred to "addicts", "substance misuse," and "overdose deaths." The officially sanctioned terms are now "people who use drugs" and "substance use." Starting in 2020, health authorities even stopped calling it an overdose crisis, preferring the term "toxic-drug crisis," the implication being that the real problem is merely the production quality of the drugs, rather than that people are addicted to them. Guy Felicella, a vocal harm reduction booster, explained in a 2023 BC government press release that the word overdose "suggests people know what they're using and how potent it is, but they're taking too much of it. That's no longer the problem."[48]

Where Canada's harm reduction saga truly veers into the surreal is health authorities going full-bore on normalizing addiction to illicit drugs at the exact same time they have brought the hammer down on legal drugs such as cigarettes and alcohol.

In 2022, Health Canada announced the decriminalization of illicit drugs in BC as a "critical step toward reducing the shame and fear associated with substance use." Only a few months later, the exact same agency was boasting that it had pioneered a new system of mandating health warnings on individual cigarettes. Canadian smokers now have to put their lips on a filter reading "poison in every puff" or "cigarettes cause impotence." The purpose of this, as Health Canada literature explains, is to increase the shame and fear associated with tobacco use, and thus, drive smokers into quitting.

Ya'ara Saks, Canada's Minister of Addictions, championed a ban on fruity flavours for vape juice, arguing that it drove teens to take up vaping.[49] At the exact same time, Saks was freely dismissing critiques that "safer supply" was funnelling freezer bags full of cheap opioids to teenagers. "A lot of what's driving the prescribed alternative debate is anchored, unfortunately … in stigma and fear," Saks told the Canadian Press in February 2024.

In the province of Ontario, an attempt to introduce alcohol into convenience stores was roundly denounced by health authorities as a potential driver of alcoholism, drunk driving, and teen drinking. "The evidence shows that as alcohol becomes more available and more affordable, you'll see increases in domestic violence, street violence, you'll see an increase in chronic diseases, various forms of cancer, increases in road crashes, youth drinking, injuries and suicides," one speaker told a July 2024 meeting of the Association of Local Public Health Agencies.[50]

That would be the same Association of Local Public Health Agencies, which had adopted a resolution two years prior of decriminalizing hard drugs and distributing more "safer supply."[51]

"One of the things that I hate is hearing policymakers say 'well, this is a complex issue.' Bullshit, it's actually very simple. If you as a community don't treat addiction faster than you create it, you will wind up with addicts all over the place," said Marshall Smith.

"It's hard, but it's not complicated."

5 | The Transing Canada Highway

When historians look back at the peak of the gender identity era, they will find plenty of countries that allowed male athletes to compete in women's sports. They'll similarly find any number of health agencies and nonprofits that embraced increasingly awkward gender-neutral terms such as "persons who menstruate" or "front hole" as a synonym for "vagina."

But only Canada had Jessica Yaniv and Kayla Lemieux.

Canada is certainly not alone among Western countries in discovering that allowing citizens to choose their own gender without question very quickly leads to a carnivalesque debacle of unintended consequences. But it's perhaps worth noting that everybody else was able to muddle through their own experiments in gender identity without shop teachers showing up to work in beach ball-sized prosthetic breasts, or estheticians being called on the carpet for refusing to wax "female testicles."

Yaniv, who now goes by the name Jessica Simpson, is best known as the trans activist who led a months-long campaign of filing human rights complaints against Vancouver-area estheticians who refused demands to wax male testicles. Subsequent court records document how this usually went.[1] Yaniv would call up an esthetician and schedule a Brazilian wax, a procedure of removing pubic hair from around the vulva. Yaniv would ask if the facility served transgender women, making sure to specify that this meant they would be performing the Brazilian wax on a set of intact male genitalia. When the esthetician said "no" (and they all said "no"), they'd hear Yaniv at the other end of the line saying "I guess I'll see you in court, bye-bye."

Yaniv would then file a complaint with the BC Human Rights Tribunal alleging that the salons had committed a "discrimination in accommodation, service, and facility."

Vexatious human rights complaints were only the tip of the Jessica Yaniv iceberg. News photographers captured the thirty-two-year-old Yaniv showing up to tribunal hearings on a mobility scooter; the need for the device was never explained.[2]

In 2019, Yaniv organized a "youth all-bodies swim" at a Langley, BC community pool that invited children as young as twelve. An event page encouraged toplessness while explicitly barring the attendance of parents. "For participant privacy and safety, parents and/or caregivers are not permitted in the event," it read.[3]

Around the same time, Yaniv applied to enter a Toronto beauty pageant for women and girls. When rejected, Yaniv immediately filed an Ontario human rights complaint seeking $10,000 to compensate for "injury to dignity and feelings."[4]

There was also the time that Yaniv got convicted of assault for attacking a journalist outside a BC courtroom, shortly after pleading not guilty to a weapons charge.[5]

There were a couple of Canadian policy changes that had brought a figure such as Yaniv into being.

For one, Canada had adopted a system of gender self-identification. Gender transitions have been a part of Canadian law ever since the 1970s, but the standing rule was that nobody could change their legal sex without a doctor's note providing proof of genital surgery.

That started to change in the 2010s, when Canadian law began to embrace the notion that someone's legal gender was what they said it was. As of this writing, eight of ten Canadian provinces now allow residents to voluntarily change their official gender; only Manitoba and Saskatchewan require a note from a doctor or psychologist.[6]

Changing the sex on one's Canadian passport, meanwhile, is one of the simplest forms produced by the Government of Canada. You just have to fill in your name, date of birth, and check a box under the line "I am requesting a Canadian travel document with the following sex or gender identifier" (the options are "male," "female" and "X").

The second major change that enabled Yaniv's rise to power was Bill C-16, a 2017 Act of Parliament that enshrined "gender identity or expression" as a protected class under both the Canadian Human Rights Act and the Criminal Code. This was the law that Yaniv would cite most regularly, sometimes with a shrug.

During a 2019 interview with conspiracy theorist Alex Jones, Yaniv was asked if estheticians should be required to "polish the johnson" of a male client identifying as a woman. "In this day and age, with the BC Human Rights Code and the Canadian Human Rights Code, if someone identifies as a woman, they have to receive those gender-affirming care services. That's the law," replied Yaniv.

* * *

Just as the international Jessica Yaniv headlines started to die down, Canada did it all again.

In September 2022, students at Oakville Trafalgar High School showed up to the first days of classes to discover that their shop teacher, Mr. Lemieux, was now Ms. Lemieux. And instead of wearing shorts and a loose-fitting polo shirt, Lemieux was now dressed in a blonde wig, nail polish, and a set of cartoonishly oversized prosthetic breasts.

Furtive cell phone photos taken by students soon captured Lemieux struggling to demonstrate a miter saw without either of the prosthetic mammaries getting caught in the equipment. The mammoth breasts were pretty obviously fetish gear. Lemieux may well have sourced them from Amazon, which carries several varieties of z-cup prosthetic breasts for between $250 and $300.

For all the ridiculousness of the Yaniv saga, the BC Human Rights Tribunal ultimately declared the whole episode a farce. Yaniv's case (which is literally called "Yaniv v. Various Waxing Salons") wrapped up in October 2019 with a decision concluding that Yaniv had transparently attempted to "target small businesses for personal financial gain."

This time around, the system sided with Lemieux. Photographs of the z-cupped teacher had only just begun to circulate around the world before the Halton District School Board chair, Margo Shuttleworth, publicly announced that it was standing behind the shop teacher's newly affirmed identity and would be "creating a safety plan" for Lemieux.[7]

Parents of Oakville students were told in an email that it was against the law for them to make an issue out of the shop teacher's new appearance. "As a school within the Halton District School Board (HDSB), Oakville Trafalgar High School recognizes the rights of students, staff, parents/guardians and community members to equitable treatment without discrimination based upon gender identity and gender expression."[8]

A year later, the Lemieux saga ended as abruptly as it had started. On the first day of classes in 2023, Lemieux showed up to work with his usual police escort, but without giant breasts, women's clothing, or even the name Kayla; he'd gone back to identifying as a man.[9]

This has led to speculation that it had all been an elaborate political stunt. Lemieux himself has remained mum on the theory. In fact, his only media interview was a bizarre sit-down with the *New York Post* in which the teacher claimed that the giant breasts were real. "My condition is classified as gigantomastia, which can also be referred to as macromastia or breast hypertrophy," said Lemieux. When reporters confronted Lemieux with photos of him exiting his apartment in a male dress, Lemieux said it was someone else.[10]

Whatever the motive in the Lemieux saga, it could not have been a more pitch-perfect tell as to the state of Canadian gender policy. Canada had just put the finishing touches on an entire national framework of allowing citizens to change their gender at will and damned if they were going to admit wrong just because a shop teacher showed up to work in fetish gear.

* * *

Unfortunately, an Ontario high school being humiliated in the eyes of the world was only among the more benign consequences of the new Canadian regime.

In spring 2024, British politics briefly ground to a halt over revelations that the United Kingdom may have just overseen one of the worst incidents of medical malpractice in a generation. The Cass Review, an official four-year probe into "gender identity services" for British minors, determined that "remarkably weak evidence" underlay virtually the entire system.

The UK had pursued an "affirmation" approach to gender care: the moment a minor said they felt like they belonged to a different gender or to no gender at all, the protocol was to accommodate the new identity without question and direct the child toward possible medical interventions. These interventions included hormone therapies and puberty blockers, both of which came with potentially irreversible consequences, such as lifelong sterility.

Hilary Cass, the respected British pediatrician who oversaw the review, concluded that there was "no good evidence on the long-term outcomes of interventions to manage gender-related distress," and that British children had been "let down" by a system that had openly ignored the "normal principles of pediatrics and mental health." Most chilling of all, Cass wrote that a lot of this had been enabled by a vicious ideological culture within British medicine. "There are few other areas of healthcare where professionals are so afraid to openly discuss their views, where people are vilified on social media and where name-calling echoes the worst bullying behaviour. This must stop," she wrote.[11]

Both the Labour and Conservative parties endorsed Cass's findings, and commentators from all sides of the political spectrum were soon in agreement that the British health system had made a terrible mistake. "Thousands of children unsure of gender identity 'let down by NHS', report finds," declared a front-page headline in *The Guardian*, the traditional standard-bearer for British progressivism.[12] A *Guardian* op-ed would later declare "the Cass review of gender identity services marks a return to reason and evidence."[13]

"The Cass Review into children's gender care should shame us all," declared the similarly left-leaning *New Statesman*.[14]

Almost none of this was noticed in Canada, even though the Cass Review provided a devastating critique of a system almost identical to Canada's own. What's more, the Cass Review was in line with a trend sweeping Europe. France, The Netherlands, Finland, Denmark, Sweden, and Norway—all of these countries, like Canada—had been at the forefront of embracing "affirming" care for gender dysphoric youth. And, one by one, they'd all come to the conclusion that they'd made a terrible mistake.

Again, Canada didn't care. If the Cass Review was mentioned at all by Canada's various medical boards or health organization, it was to denounce it out of hand. The Canadian Paediatric Society said so explicitly.

In 2024, a public letter signed by three Canadian pediatricians urged the society to adopt the "cautious approach" recommended by Cass and banish puberty blockers to the "context of research." The society responded immediately, saying the Cass Review, a four-year inquiry whose final report came to 388 pages, was nothing more than "a critique, authored by a single individual."[15]

As such, the "affirmation approach" would continue. In the society's most recent "gender affirmation" guidelines, Canadian pediatricians are told that their patients could well be transgender if they demonstrate "a strong preference for playmates of the other gender," show a "dislike" of their genitals, or favour "the toys, games, or activities stereotypically used or engaged in by the other gender."[16]

Pediatrics is far from the only realm of Canadian life that has gone all-in on the notion that someone's gender is what they say it is. Starting in 2017, Canadian prisons started placing inmates based entirely on their self-identified gender. "Offenders will be placed according to their gender identity or expression in a men's or a women's institution, if that is their preference, regardless of their sex (i.e., anatomy) or the gender/sex marker on their identification documents," reads Corrections Canada's official regulations.[17]

As of a 2022 count by Corrections Canada, fourteen offenders identifying as trans-women had requested transfer to a women's prison. Zero offenders identifying as trans-men had requested the reverse.[18] According to a 2022 *Toronto Sun* report, one of the successful transferees was a killer jailed in 1995 for murdering a female upstairs neighbour and then committing necrophilia against the victim's corpse. Incarcerated as a man, the killer now went by the name Catherine Lynn.[19] Sources at the Grand Valley Institution women's prison told the *Toronto Sun* that Lynn was one of their inmates.

Any Canadian man looking to save money on auto insurance now needs only to report to a government registrar and declare that they're now a woman. In 2018, CBC interviewed an Alberta man identified only as "David" who saved $1,100 on his auto insurance premiums by simply asking the provincial government to change his birth certificate from male to female. Overnight, his annual premiums dropped from $4,517 to $3,423.[20] His widely circulated Reddit post stated: "I now pay $1,100 less for auto insurance. I won. The end."

Vancouver Rape Relief and Women's Shelter, Canada's oldest rape crisis centre, was stripped of city funding in 2019 after it refused demands to start admitting women based on identity rather than biology.[21] The centre's argument was that it was a place for women recovering from sexual abuse, and a self-ID policy would allow male predators to access the facility simply by claiming to be female. "Trans women are women … I can't support (organizations) who exclude them," said a city councillor, Christine Boyle, justifying her support for the defunding in a social media post.

Ever since, Vancouver Rape Relief has remained a steady target of vandalism and threats framing them as a bastion of transphobia. In quick succession in 2019, they had a dead rat nailed to their door and "KILL TERFS" scrawled across their windows, the latter a reference to the term "trans-exclusionary radical feminist."

Lawyers in Ontario legal proceedings must now provide the preferred pronouns of anyone they introduce to the court, be it a client, a witness, or themselves. For the first 157 years of the Ontario court system, just a name and title were sufficient. But now, as per an order by Ontario Chief Justice Sharon Nicklas, judges should be explicitly told whether the person being introduced is a woman, a man, or something else.[22]

In 2023, the Canadian Armed Forces became the first military on earth to require men's bathrooms to be stocked with tampons and other menstrual products. It was all part of a sweeping federal guidance applying to any federally regulated workplace, including military bases. In a guidance that strenuously avoided the use of the term "woman," employers were told that "menstrual products must be in all toilet rooms, regardless of their marked genders."[23]

Gender identity has also affected Canadian policing. In 2023, Metro Vancouver Transit Police issued a conspicuously gender-neutral request for assistance in identifying the suspect behind a sexual assault at a SkyTrain station. Despite semen from the suspect being recovered from the scene, police refused to identify a gender. "The video evidence shows someone who … would appear female, who is female presenting, but the physical evidence is that of a genetic male," a police spokeswoman would be quoted as saying on the feminist news website Reduxx.[24]

When BC resident Kevin "Bear" Henry became the subject of a missing person's alert in 2021, police were careful to only use Henry's preferred pronouns of they/them in official statements. "They have short brown hair and green eyes," read a police alert about the missing individual (who was eventually found alive after two months).[25]

Across all levels of Canadian government, a small army of bureaucrats is now employed to strike out any language that might hint at the existence of a gender binary. The federal Department of Justice has published an entire guide to civil servants on how to write legislation, orders and government communiques in such a way that men or women are never specifically referenced. "In the past, the doublet 'he or she' was … recommended as a more inclusive alternative to the default masculine 'he.' It is no longer recommended because it implies a binary conception of gender that may not include some gender-diverse individuals," it reads.[26]

BC has a team tasked with deleting "outdated gendered language" from all of its laws and statutes, no matter how obscure. In one twelve-month period, the team identified 741 "outdated" phrases and words across 138 regulations, each of which needed to be corrected with its own individual amendment signed by the province's lieutenant governor.[26] One of these was an update to the Milk Industry Standards. In place of a line requiring dairy workers to "wash and dry his or her hands," it now reads that farms must "ensure that the bulk tank milk grader's hands are clean by washing and drying them."

Canadian public health agencies have similarly gone to great lengths to omit gendered language, even when it comes to extremely gendered activities such as pregnancy. When the Public Health Agency of Canada released its guidance on COVID-19 vaccines and pregnancy, the document referred only to "people who are pregnant" or "pregnant persons."[27]

Many of these changes were implemented quietly, with most Canadians only noticing a change once they were looking at census forms implying that their sex had been "assigned at birth."

Take the example of males in women's prisons: the whole policy followed a knee-jerk promise by the prime minister after an activist had requested as much during a press conference. At a January 2017 town hall in Kingston, Ontario, an audience member asked Trudeau to end the "torture of transgender inmates" in the Canadian prison system. "Will you do your best to ensure that trans women are put in … a prison more appropriate to their gender identity?" asked the audience member. Trudeau replied that "trans rights are human rights" and that he would be looking into it as soon as possible. Within hours, Public Safety Canada confirmed that a policy change was already underway and the Correctional Service of Canada would be "reviewing trans inmate's placement requests on a case-by-case basis." [28]

* * *

Linda Blade can recall the precise moment when gender identity, something she'd never previously thought too much about, suddenly became her defining professional issue.

In 2018, Blade was president of Track and Field Alberta. She was in a meeting with all the various regional heads of Athletics Canada, the sport's central governing body. At the top of the agenda, they were told of a new nationwide policy under which eligibility for men's and women's sports would now be based on identity; if an athlete was born male and had a male body but identified as female, they had to play with the girls. "I was stunned. I couldn't believe it," said Blade.

Athletics, in particular, is a sport of records: fastest time, highest jump, and furthest javelin throw. And Blade knew that every single women's record could easily be shattered by a male, even if just a boy competing at the high school level.

In fact, for Blade to earn a doctorate in Kinesiology from Simon Fraser University, she wrote a thesis plotting the differences in tissue development between boys and girls as they approach adulthood. "Every record on the books shows that males have dominant performances over females," she said.[29]

Blade's objections yielded only a room full of people "looking down at their hands" or telling her she risked violating anti-discrimination laws if she didn't go along with the new policy.

At the time, there hadn't been a conspicuous example of transgender women demolishing the competition in a women's sports category. It wasn't until 2022, for instance, that women's swimming in the United States would witness the rise of Lia Thomas, a middle-ranked collegiate athlete who began shattering women's competitions shortly after identifying as female.

It's entirely possible that Athletics Canada was simply hoping that wouldn't happen in its jurisdiction. But Blade described a 2018 dinner in Calgary with the head of the organization where she laid out her legal case against the self-ID measure. If Athletics Canada was trying to evade an anti-discrimination lawsuit by transgenderizing its eligibility rules, Blade said it risked an even larger legal liability from biological women arguing that the measure violated their sex-based rights. "He might have been joking, but he said 'girls wouldn't do that,'" she said.

It was the beginning of Blade becoming the outspoken head of an effort to abolish gender identity guidelines in women's sports, a movement that has just started to gain serious traction as this book goes to press.

In October 2024, Blade's home province of Alberta introduced the Fairness in Safety and Sport Act, Canada's first legislation to entrench "biological female-only divisions" in sport. Blade was also in the room in summer 2023 when the Conservative Party of Canada introduced a resolution pledging itself to the "privacy of single-sex spaces ... and the benefits of women-only categories."

"I'm quite sure that the tide is turning, because you can't lie forever," said Blade. "And it is a lie; it's a lie that a man can just become a woman because of some words they said."

* * *

Canadians aren't particularly bothered if a close family member starts identifying as trans. A 2023 poll by the Angus Reid Institute asked respondents what they would do if one of their own children started identifying as a different gender. More than two-thirds (69 percent) said they would accept it without question (with 12 percent saying they would "enthusiastically" accept it).[30] An Ipsos poll from a few months later similarly found 74 percent of Canadians agreeing that "transgender people should be protected from discrimination in employment, housing, and access to businesses."[31] This was one of the highest results among twenty-six developed nations surveyed by Ipsos. This is to be expected for a country that has been an early adopter of gay rights going back to the 1960s.

Canada decriminalized homosexuality in 1967, at a time when sodomy was still illegal across much of Europe and the United States. Homosexuals have been able to serve openly in the Canadian military since 1992—nineteen years before the United States adopted a similar policy. Canada was such an outlier in its 2005 legalization of same-sex marriage that it even spawned a miniature economic boom as Canada briefly became a destination for wealthy gay couples denied marriage rights in any other major economy.

For a time in the early 2010s, a Conservative Canadian government was pushing the virtues of gay rights to the wider world. When the African nation of Uganda looked to pass a draconian law that included penalties for anyone who didn't report their gay neighbours, it was Conservative Prime Minister Stephen Harper who was pulling Ugandan President Yoweri Museveni aside at international summits to warn that there could be dire consequences if the bill went forward. "When I was at the Commonwealth conference, what was [Stephen Harper] talking about? The gays," Museveni told BBC News in 2010.[32]

The compelling pitch underlying all of Canada's embrace of gay rights was that the sex lives of Canadians was nobody's business but their own. As Canada's justice minister (and future prime minister), Pierre Trudeau, said upon Canada's decriminalization of homosexuality in 1967: "The view we take is, there's no place for the state in the bedrooms of the nation."

In 2005, Prime Minister Paul Martin used similar language in defending the bill that would legalize same-sex marriage across the country. "Nothing has been lost or sacrificed by the majority in extending full rights to the minority," he told the House of Commons.

But it's on the issue of gender identity that this bargain has suddenly spun apart as Canadians realized that their government's vision of trans liberation came with some pretty hefty unintended consequences. While the Lemieux and Yaniv cases made headlines, it was still easy to dismiss them as fringe dwellers. It was the issue of gender affirmation in schools that Canada got its first look at a policy that almost everyone agreed had gone too far.

The spark came out of the small Atlantic province of New Brunswick. In the summer of 2023, New Brunswick Premier Blaine Higgs suddenly came out publicly against Policy 713, the province's "Sexual Orientation and Gender Identity" guidelines for public schools.

Only three years prior, Higg's own government had introduced the guidelines, which effectively enshrined a "student's right to self-identify." Now, Higgs wanted to reverse a clause of Policy 713 that required teachers to adopt a student's new gender identity upon request while keeping the entire thing a secret from their parents. If parents object to a child's new identity, "a plan will be put in place to support the student in managing the use of the preferred name in the learning environment." And there was no minimum age for Policy 713; it was the same deal for kindergartners as for high schoolers.

The move was almost universally condemned by the media as well as the New Brunswick Medical Society. A good chunk of Higgs' cabinet resigned in protest. But when the issue was put to the polls, the people were with Higgs. By a long shot. The same Canadians who supported trans equality by margins of more than 70 percent were also virulently opposed to the idea of schools facilitating the social transitioning of supposedly gender-confused children without their parent's knowledge.

A survey by SecondStreet.org at the time explained Policy 713 to a representative sample of Canadian adults and asked if they would keep the clause to socially transition children without parental knowledge. Only 18 percent said "yes," with 57 percent agreeing with Higgs that parents should be looped in.[33]

The Angus Reid Institute found even starker numbers on "pronoun policies" in schools. An August 2023 survey returned the results that a mere 14 percent of Canadians agreed with the notion that on issues of gender identity, "parents should neither be informed nor have a say."[34] Everyone else in the survey was of mixed opinion as to whether a parent should be allowed to kibosh their child's request for new pronouns, but 78 percent said it couldn't be done in secret.

More surprising still was the revelation that Higgs was describing a policy that was already the law of the land across most of the country. Just as in New Brunswick, everywhere from Ontario to Alberta to BC to Ontario had quietly adopted policies requiring schools to secretly affirm new identities, names, and pronouns upon request.

As early as 2021, instances emerged of Canadian parents discovering that schools had been socially transitioning their children in secret. The *National Post* profiled one example of a Calgary grade six class being told the new name and pronouns of a classmate, and then being sworn to secrecy about revealing the identity to the child's parents. "This upset me so much," said a parent of one of the children. "Kids were being taught to lie to parents."[35]

In the early 2010s, Meghan Murphy was a women's studies post-graduate and self-described socialist with a job at the left-wing opinion site Rabble.ca. It was a vantage point from which she was able to see the first stirrings of what would become the Canadian gender movement, built around the notions that legal gender should be based on self-identification rather than biological markers such as genitalia; that gender was not a binary; that someone with a penis could be a lesbian; or that any women-only space, be it a bathroom or rape shelter, was inherently anti-trans.

"I had the privilege, I suppose, of being in this radical feminist blogosphere and being engaged in all these arguments that were not mainstream," she said. As such, Murphy was probably one of the first women in Canada to experience something that's now pretty common: seeing a term like "pregnant person" used in place of "woman" and getting an uneasy feeling.[36]

This would ultimately come into the open with a 2015 column in which Murphy criticized a nude photospread of transgender actress Laverne Cox published in Allure magazine. Specifically, she objected to the popular notion that the images were "empowering" or an example of "radical self-acceptance." "If women or transwomen were truly allowed to love themselves, I doubt they'd be spending thousands and thousands of dollars sculpting their bodies in order to look like some cartoonish version of 'woman,'" she wrote.[37]

It was the article that began Murphy's rapid exile from progressive society. Rabble was barraged with demands for her firing. Coworkers refused to speak to her. "People would tell my boyfriend 'you can't bring Meghan,'" she said.

She would resign from the site the next year when it pulled a column of hers objecting to the adoption of the term "menstruator" by the group Planned Parenthood. "It is unfortunate that you do not see the problems around the erasure of trans male identity in the piece," she was told by her editor.[38] Two years later, Murphy would be permanently banned from the social media site Twitter for referring to Jessica Yaniv using the pronoun "him."

Murphy now lives part of the year in Mexico, runs a podcast and the website Feminist Current and will occasionally make public appearances under extremely high-security conditions.

Venues that host talks by Murphy can usually expect campaigns of harassing phone calls, legal threats, vandalism, and protesters attempting to block the doors. As a result, anytime she makes an appearance, the location is kept secret from registered attendees until a few hours prior and staffed up with perimeter security.

And yet, even for someone who had an early view on the extremes of the Canadian gender identity movement, Murphy said she still didn't anticipate how far it was going to go.

"I don't think anyone could have predicted what is going on now," she said. "I didn't realize it was going to get this crazy; I didn't think it was going to be about transitioning minors."

6 | A Whiff of the Orwellian

Margaret Atwood easily ranks as Canada's leading expert on imagining nightmarish dystopias. She is the author of *The Handmaid's Tale*, which depicts the United States as a totalitarian theocracy where women are oppressed chattel forced to bear children for the elite. She is also the author of the 2003 bestseller *Oryx and Crake*, which features a bleak post apocalyptic world destroyed by greedy biotechnology corporations.

So Canadians took notice, in March 2024, when Atwood told them that their own government appeared to be flirting with dystopia. On her X.com account, Atwood posted a link to a column in the British magazine *The Spectator* entitled "Trudeau's Orwellian online harms bill."

"If this account of the bill is true, it's Lettres de Cachet all over again," wrote Atwood, making reference to a practice in pre-revolutionary France where subjects could be jailed indefinitely on the orders of the King.[1] She added that the bill could be a magnet for "revenge false accusations" as well as "thought-crime stuff." The latter being a reference to 1984, the George Orwell novel depicting a totalitarian future in which the very act of having an opinion contrary to the ruling party is considered a crime.

The legislation in question, Bill C-63, was pitched by its Liberal sponsors as a salve against internet hate and online extremism. But a cursory reading of the text revealed measures that went well beyond a good-faith effort to crack on racist internet comments. It imposed one of the democratic world's first-ever life sentences for a speech crime. Anybody convicted of promoting genocide was "liable to imprisonment for life." It also empowered law enforcement to imprison Canadians on the mere suspicion that they were going to say something hateful. If there are "reasonable grounds" to assume that someone is thinking of committing a hate crime offence, Bill C-63 allowed judges to sentence them to as much as twelve months of preemptive house arrest.

The Spectator was not the only foreign publication to notice Bill C-63 as evidence of a looming Canadian censorship regime. *Forbes* also made reference to 1984 in its review of Bill C-63. "Free speech is under such threat in Canada it would make Orwell blush," declared the magazine.[2] "No free speech? New 'Orwellian' law endorsed by Trudeau government could imprison people for life," wrote the *Times of India*.[3] Multiple publications, from *The Atlantic* to the *Deseret News*, wrote that Canada was dabbling in "pre-crime," a reference to the 2002 film *Minority Report*, which depicts a future in which criminals are jailed before they commit crimes.

Amnesty International, which usually has an easy time endorsing curbs on "harmful" speech, thought Bill C-63 went a bit too far.[4] In a public letter, it said the legislation was tainted by "disproportionate punishments that risk chilling legitimate speech."

And Bill C-63 was only the latest in a suite of federal legislation undermining free expression in Canada. There was the Online Streaming Act, which imposed government content controls on streaming services such as Netflix or YouTube. And then came the Online News Act, which required web giants such as Facebook and Google to divert tens of millions in revenue to media outlets whose links were shared on their platforms.

All the while, Parliament has been moving forward on a Senate bill that would enable regulators to bring the hammer down on any website that makes sexually explicit content available online, a category that includes everything from social media to search engines to Archive.org. These bills have rapidly pushed Canada toward owning the most regulated internet in the free world. And if there's one throughline to all the legislation, it's that they were all pitched as targeted measures to address uncontroversial problems.

The Online Streaming Act was framed as a simple bid for "cultural sovereignty."[5] The federal government was controlling online streaming content merely to boost the visibility of Canadian-made media.

The preamble to the Online News Act claims it is a mechanism to "enhance fairness in the Canadian digital news marketplace."

The official name of the Senate bill is the "Protecting Young Persons from Exposure to Pornography Act."

But take a closer look at the actual text of the three bills, and they're all incredibly broad and layered with unintended consequences.

The Online Streaming Act adopts an extremely specific definition of what qualifies as "Canadian content" and requires streaming websites to punish anything that doesn't meet the standard. For scores of Canadian YouTubers, this has imposed whole new latticeworks of paperwork and red tape and meant that they risk delisting if they so much as appear with a non-Canadian co-host.[6]

The Online News Act was so onerous that Facebook simply shut down its Canadian news. Any attempt to put a news link in a Facebook post yields only the alert "in response to Canadian government legislation, news content can't be shared."

The Senate pornography bill effectively gives Ottawa the power to impose ID verification on any corner of the internet carrying racy pictures. In an extreme example, Google could face fines or government shutdown unless it requires users to first verify their identity using a federally-approved facial recognition service. Michael Geist, a University of Ottawa professor who is one of Canada's leading internet policy scholars, has called it "the most dangerous Canadian internet bill you've never heard of."[7]

Just as with Margaret Atwood's callout of Bill C-63, there were any number of high-profile critics willing to point out that these were shoddily written bills that would immediately yield unintended consequences if made law. But, time after time, critics have been told everything will be fine.

Justice Minister Arif Virani introduced Bill C-63 to the House of Commons by stating "it does not undermine freedom of expression. It strengthens freedom of expression by allowing all people to participate safely in online discussions."

The authors of the Online Streaming Act repeatedly promised that it would not apply to social media. But as soon as it passed, Canada's federal telecom regulator mandated that everyone from Facebook to Reddit had to register with authorities or risk sanction.[8]

If Bill C-63 was uniquely able to inspire international headlines, it's mostly because it was so obviously beyond the pale. But if the Canadian federal government had suddenly become comfortable with proposing something as draconian as jailing citizens for "likely" hate speech, it's largely a reflection of a Canadian censorship framework that has been gaining ground for quite some time.

The story of Canada's last ten years is that you can quietly curb a whole bunch of free expression before Margaret Atwood notices.

* * *

There are few Canadian stories as bizarre as the meteoric rise of psychologist Jordan Peterson. And it happened almost entirely because of an otherwise obscure amendment to Canadian human rights law.

As recently as 2015, Peterson was one among a dozen or so tenured professors in the psychology department of the University of Toronto. His single book, *Maps of Meaning*, had sold a scattering of copies before being consigned to the long-term storage areas of university libraries. On the rare occasion that Peterson was ever quoted in the press, it was usually for some weekend feature about pop psychology. When a Canadian press reporter asked Peterson why Furbys were cute, the professor had explained that the toys were emblems of "neoteny," juvenile features on an adult form.[9]

By the end of the decade, Peterson was filling stadiums around the world. He had authored one of the best-selling self-help books of the twenty-first century and had a social media reach rivaled by few academics anywhere. Fans and enemies alike were referring to him unironically as a kind of "messiah." (It's even the name of his unauthorized biography, *Savage Messiah*).

It's a rock star career arc that basically never happens to fifty-something psychology professors, much less a Canadian one who has openly acknowledged that his voice sounds like Kermit the Frog. And the hinge point between those two versions of Jordan Peterson was a dispute over a seemingly minor update to the Canadian Human Rights Code.

In 2016, the House of Commons approved an amendment to the Code adding "gender identity" and "gender expression" to the list of traits shielded from discrimination. The bill had basically been rubber-stamped through Parliament. It passed 248 to 40, and the only real objection to its passage was that it was unnecessary. In the Conservative critique of the bill, Alberta MP Michael Cooper argued that it was already illegal to discriminate against transgendered Canadians. "Bill C-16 would not add or take anything away," he said.

Peterson saw it differently. In a series of low-production YouTube videos that quickly went viral, the professor explained that Canada was effectively looking to quash the speech of anyone who expressed the view that gender stuck to a clear male/female binary. "I think some of the things I am teaching may now be illegal to even say," he explained in one.[10]

But what really put Peterson in the international spotlight was his assertion that the law would require him to employ the preferred pronouns of students and staff. One slip-up on forgetting that an undergrad went by "they," "ze" or "zhir," and he'd face professional sanctions, fines, or worse. "These words are at the vanguard of a post-modern, radical leftist ideology that I detest, and which is, in my professional opinion, frighteningly similar to the Marxist doctrines that killed at least 100 million people in the 20th century," Peterson wrote in the *National Post* at the height of the controversy.[11]

If all this seemed like an overreaction to a four-word amendment to the Human Rights Code, Peterson was up against a Canadian system that is particularly aggressive in how it enforces said human rights code. And it's this system that has made Canada an increasingly easy place to chill speech or control behaviour.

The Canadian Human Rights Code isn't just a statement of values like the United Nation's Universal Declaration of Human Rights. Its tenets are enforced by a 300-member, $30 million-a-year Canadian Human Rights Commission with awesome powers to investigate violators and refer them to the Canadian Human Rights Tribunal for punishment.

The process goes thusly: if you feel you've been discriminated against, you file a complaint to the commission and if it deems the complaint worthy of investigation, it takes it from there. The commission shoulders the entire cost of investigating the complaint and putting it before the tribunal for adjudication. Meanwhile, the complainant's participation in this whole process is minimal; they don't even have to be in the country.

And there are fourteen of these kinds of human rights enforcers. The Canadian Human Rights Commission deals with complaints in areas of federal jurisdiction, such as aviation or the banking sector. And then each province and territory has its own human rights body to deal with everything else. Sometimes there's a commission/tribunal combo. Sometimes, as in the case of BC, complaints are made directly through the tribunal.

They are all ostensibly independent of one another and follow their own specific codes, but in practice they're all basically the same. Within weeks of Bill C-16 adding "gender identity" to the Canadian Human Rights Act, it was then written into every other province-level code that didn't yet have it.

The tribunals have many of the powers of a court but without the checks and responsibilities of one. The burden of proof is lower, the agency acts as both prosecutor and judge, and there is basically no cost for filing a complaint.

If you sue an employer for breach of contract in Canada, you've got to find a lawyer, file a statement of claim, and cover the cost and time of litigating your cases before a court. If you want to accuse that employer of being a racist, all you have to do is fill out a form. The employer will likely have to get a lawyer to defend themselves from the resulting tribunal action, but you don't.

This was the imbalance exploited by Jessica Yaniv. To call estheticians onto the carpet for refusing to wax testicles, all Yaniv had to do was spend a few minutes clicking through the BC Human Rights Tribunal's online complaints form. The immigrant women targeted by the complaints (and they were all immigrant women) were on their own. The Calgary-based Justice Centre for Constitutional Freedoms took up their case pro bono.

Despite arguably becoming the most brazen abuser of the human rights tribunal system in Canadian history, Yaniv's only punishment for all this was a $6,000 fine, a fraction of the damages the process meted out to Yaniv's victims. According to the Justice Centre for Constitutional Freedoms, the stress of the process caused some of their clients to shut down their esthetician business altogether.[12]

After all this, Yaniv was still allowed to continue making complaints against estheticians who refused to wax male testicles. After Yaniv found a new esthetician to target only three months after the first batch of complaints was dismissed, the tribunal responded that it couldn't pursue the complaint until the $6,000 fine was paid up.

Nobody else except Canada enforces anti-discrimination laws this way. In most of the world, any discrimination law is enforced through the regular court system, rather than via quasi-judicial tribunals that are scandalously prone to abuse. Even in countries such as Australia or the United Kingdom that have adopted elements of the Canadian system, they've stopped short of giving their tribunals broad powers to prosecute and punish violators. Australia has a Human Rights Commission, but the body is more of an impartial mediator. Australians can file human rights complaints just the same as in Canada, but all they're going to get is "conciliation," a kind of arbitration process in which the complainant expresses their feelings to their alleged discriminator and requests voluntary redress. "The conciliator's role is to help both sides talk to each other and try to reach an agreement," reads an online guide.[13] The commission is not able to levy fines or compel apologies; that all has to be sought through a court if conciliation doesn't work out.

The Canadian human rights apparatus often needs only the word of the complainant to plunge a defendant into a ruinous odyssey of investigations, hearings, and compelled remedies.

Jordan Peterson hasn't been the only one to note the awesome and largely unnoticed powers of the Canadian tribunal system to control speech and shape behaviour. Cheri Di Novo is an Ontario politician who was instrumental in adding "gender expression" and "gender identity" into the Ontario Human Rights Code in 2012. The move made Ontario the first province to enshrine gender expression as a protected class. In a particularly illuminating passage of her 2021 autobiography, Di Novo says that the amendment passed only because nobody realized how disruptive it was going to be.

Overnight, Ontarians didn't just risk a human rights complaint for ignoring someone's preferred pronouns but for doing anything that didn't conform to a new legal reality in which someone's gender was whatever they said it was. As Di Novo wrote, "everything from identity cards to prison practice" was now different. "I don't believe for an instant that the government realized the scope of that one change to the Human Rights Code. I'm glad they didn't look too closely."[14]

So it's perhaps no surprise that many of the most notable challenges to free speech in Canada have sprung from a human rights commission or tribunal. In 2006, *Maclean's* magazine was hit with human rights complaints in BC, Ontario and at the federal level urging the publication to be sanctioned for publishing a book excerpt by right-wing author Mark Steyn. The future belongs to Islam, an excerpt from Steyn's book America Alone, argued that Western countries were set to be demographically overwhelmed by Islamists. The Canadian Islamic Congress argued in its complaint that the article spread hatred against Muslims, contrary to Canadian human rights law, and *Maclean's* would ultimately find itself in front of tribunal hearings in both Ontario and BC.[15]

In 2021, Quebec comedian Mike Ward had to appeal a human rights complaint all the way to the Supreme Court after he was slapped with a $42,000 fine for telling an offensive joke. It was over a routine in which Ward mocked Jérémy Gabriel, a well-known Quebec child singer with bone deformities known as "Le Petit Jérémy." In a televised special, Ward described defending Gabriel's poor singing to his friends, only to realize his disability wasn't terminal. "I didn't stop defending him until, five years later, Christ, he's not dead!" Ward says in the routine's major laugh line.

In both the Steyn and Ward cases, free speech ultimately prevailed. The Supreme Court ruled in Ward's favour, and the various complaints against *Macleans* were dismissed, albeit at considerable expense.

Nevertheless, the free speech protections that clicked into place in both instances may already be gone. In Ward's case, a single vote secured his victory at the Supreme Court. The decision was 5-4, meaning that four of the justices thought Ward should have paid the $42,000 for telling an off-colour joke. In their dissent, the four justices all took Ward's jokes literally, implying that the comedian had essentially given a speech arguing "that it would be too burdensome for society" to accept the existence of Jérémy Gabriel, "and that ultimately society would be better off if he were dead."

"The mere fact that it provoked laughter, or that the speech was delivered in performance, does not change Mr. Ward's message," they wrote.

Only two years after the decision, the Supreme Court lost one of the justices that had ruled in Wards' favour. Russell Brown resigned amid allegations that he had gotten into a scuffle at an Arizona resort and was soon replaced with a new appointee selected by Prime Minister Justin Trudeau.

In the Steyn case, many of the institutions that came to the defence of *Maclean's* magazine have now changed their tune on free speech. At the time, the BC Civil Liberties Association (BCCLA) sided with *Maclean's* as an intervenor in their BC hearings, issuing a submission to the tribunal saying that the case was the evidence that they had become "overly expansive" in their mandate.[16]

Of late, the BCCLA has been doing the opposite: actively campaigning to shut down speech. In 2017, when a group calling itself the Worldwide Coalition Against Islam organized a rally at Vancouver City Hall, the BCCLA didn't defend its right to free speech. Rather, it organized a counter-rally to shout it down. "Silence cannot be our option. Those who promote hateful racist, Islamophobic, and anti-immigrant ideologies could take muteness as indifference or even approval," read a BCCLA statement at the time.[17]

The Canadian Association of Journalists also sided with *Maclean's* and sent their counsel to argue that the complaint was unconstitutional.[18] Nowadays, the Canadian Association of Journalists' willingness to defend a controversial column about Muslims might be answered by the fact that one of its main projects today is meticulous cataloguing of Canadian journalists by race and then sounding the alarm if ratios aren't perfectly representative of the broader society. Its 2023 report found that Asians and Black journalists were "underrepresented," while white, Middle Eastern, and Indigenous journalists were "overrepresented." "The vast majority of Canadian newsrooms are not representative of the communities they serve," read a conclusion.[19]

To cap it all of, in 2019, the Toronto-based Centre for Free Expression marked the twelfth anniversary of the case by stating that Steyn and *Maclean's* should have been censored. "Islamophobic speech," they wrote, should fall "outside the scope of free speech protection."[20]

Beneath these big cases has come a steady trickle of smaller instances of Canadians being fined by a human rights tribunal for something they said or being told that a statement they made is against the law.

When a teaching assistant at Wilfrid Laurier University showed undergraduates a clip from a panel show featuring Jordan Peterson, she was called before university administrators and told that its content broke the law. "You have to think about the kind of teaching climate that you're creating … these arguments are counter to the Canadian Human Rights Code," she was told by her supervising professor in a recording of the meeting.[21]

In 2019, the BC Human Rights Tribunal levied $55,000 in penalties against a religious activist who distributed literature branding a transgender politician as being immoral for embracing a "transvestite lifestyle."[22]

As this book goes to press, the small Ontario town of Emo was hit with $15,000 in fines by the Ontario Human Rights Tribunal for voting down a request from a local LGBT group to issue a proclamation for Pride Month. During a 2020 town council meeting discussing the proposed proclamation, Emo's mayor was recorded as saying "there's no flags being flown for the straight people." For the tribunal, that was enough to declare that the rejected proclamation constituted "discrimination under the Code." The town was required to pay $10,000, the mayor $5,000, and both the mayor and the town's chief administration officer were ordered to undergo mandatory "human rights" training.[23]

* * *

When the events of the Watergate Scandal blew into the open in 1972, more than a few Canadian observers said that if a similar scandal were ever to hit their own country, nobody would ever hear about it. Watergate involved revelations that US President Richard Nixon had ordered a break-in at the headquarters of his campaign opponents and then overseen an elaborate cover-up when the burglars were caught.

Washington Post journalists Bob Woodward and Carl Bernstein, instrumental in exposing the early stages of the scandal, were able to rely on a culture of transparency that just didn't exist in Canada: civil servants and political staffers who spoke to journalists by default; public records that were comparatively easy to obtain and trace; police who were strenuous in publicizing the details of investigations. "Based on the record of Canadian journalism, no Canadian newspaper would have touched the kind of information which led to the *Post's* Pulitzer Prize," wrote political journalist Maurice Cutler in 1973.[24]

When a US Senate committee began probing the scandal, the *Financial Post* wrote of the average Canadian's shock at seeing how readily US lawmakers were able to dredge up "secrets of the sort that any government would want to hide."

Canada's less open society can probably best be summed up by the text of its Charter of Rights and Freedoms, which opens with a warning to Canadians that any freedom can be curbed. Section 2 guarantees freedom of expression, but Section 1 notes that this freedom is subject to "reasonable limits prescribed by law as can be demonstrably justified in a free and democratic society." And Canadian government agencies are quite comfortable in outlining their view that speech is a thing best controlled.

The Ontario Human Rights Commission's online explainer about "gender identity and pronouns" has an entire section reminding the reader that they don't have freedom of expression and must choose their words carefully. "The words that are chosen matter: the more harmful the words, the further they are from the core values of freedom of expression," it reads, adding that the "vulnerability of the group affected by the speech" could determine whether it's illegal or not.

Canadian broadcasting, similarly, is accustomed to a short leash from government regulators. Ever since the 1970s, Canadian radio and TV broadcasting have been subject to stringent quotas on Canadian content. The average Canadian has heard utterly disproportionate quantities of Anne Murray and Gordon Lightfoot for the simple reason that if FM stations don't play a minimum selection of Canadian songs, they'll be stripped of their licenses. Not even X-rated TV channels are immune. In 2014, the gay porn channel Maleflixxx was threatened by federal regulators for failing to broadcast a minimum of 8.5 hours per day of Canadian gay porn.[25]

The internet was different. What it did to Canada was to introduce a sphere where none of these controls existed. A place where a Canadian could act like an American. And this is perhaps why Canadians were able to thrive on it more than most. Many of the world's most well-known Canadians are now YouTubers. The Toronto-based YouTube channel Sierra & Rhia FAM, which chronicles the quotidian adventures of a four-member family, has 26 million subscribers. For context, the most-watched broadcast in Canadian history, the 2010 Olympic men's gold medal hockey game, only had 16.6 million viewers.

By seeking to bring the Canadian internet to heel with content controls, limits on news, and sanctions on speech, the federal government is actually just bringing Canada's online world in line with everything else.

It wasn't until Ottawa started threatening life sentences for speech crimes that its democratic peers began noticing that their Canadian cousin had developed a bit of a censorship problem. But this is arguably the culmination of a culture that has always been comfortable with speech controls and has been slowly lowering itself into a warm bath of censorship over the past twenty years.

This can be seen in the private members' bills that have been put before the House of Commons at the same time as Trudeau's so-called "pre-crime" bill. The left-wing New Democratic Party put up a bill that prescribed jail for anyone who "promoted" the use of fossil fuels,[26] and another that prescribed jail for anyone who spoke positively of Indian residential schools.[27] Neither had a realistic chance of passing. But a generation ago, Canada's left-wing standard-bearer would have been the last to propose bans on speech. In fact, it was only been eleven years prior when, in response to a pending anti-terrorism bill, an NDPer rose to critique the legislation with a lengthy defence of free expression. "The main protection of a free society is its ability to accommodate and tolerate diversity, its ability to respect rights for all, its ability to protect free speech, and its respect for those fundamental legal traditions that say that no one should go to jail who has not committed a specific criminal act," said Randall Garrison, shadow minister of public safety.

All the while, Jordan Peterson was right.

In 2021, five years after "gender expression" was added to Canada's various human rights codes, a BC restaurant was punished for the new offence of misgendering. The complainant was Jessie Nelson, a server at an Italian restaurant in Gibsons, the small BC town best known as the shooting location for the show *The Beachcombers.* Nelson, going by the pronouns they/them, took issue with a bar manager using the moniker "sweetheart" and "honey" and was soon suggesting in staff meetings that the restaurant should eschew any gendered language in speaking to customers. Four weeks into the job, after a heated confrontation with the bar manager over pronouns issue, Nelson was fired with the explanation "part of the problem is making sure you vibe with the team."

The BC Human Rights Tribunal disagreed, ruled that "pronouns are a fundamental part of a person's identity," hit the restaurant with a $30,000 fine, and ordered it to draw up a pronouns policy.

Nelson's lawyer, Adrienne Smith, called the decision a "signal" to other employers: "Correct pronouns for individuals are not optional."[28]

7 | What if We Just Stopped Jailing Criminals?

Two days after Christmas, 2022, Ontario Provincial Police Const. Grzegorz "Greg" Pierzchala pulled up on a vehicle in the ditch near Brantford, Ontario. Pierzchala knew nothing about the car or its occupants and was presumably pulling over to offer assistance. He was fatally shot in an ambush-style attack within moments of exiting his patrol vehicle.

Pierzchala was among eight Canadian police officers to be murdered on duty in the span of just seven months, an all-time record in a country that usually only saw one or two peace officers murdered per year.[1] His death came within a wave of tragedies committed by suspects on bail or early release. Pierzchala's death would end up prompting a joint statement from Canada's four largest police associations demanding bail reform. Ontario Provincial Police Commissioner Thomas Carrique would directly attribute Pierzchala's death to a lax federal approach to bail.[2]

But probably the most troubling aspect of Pierzchala's killing is that it almost certainly would not have happened if the suspect had been Caucasian. Not because the suspect's race prompted him to shoot a police officer, but because it gave him lighter treatment at the hands of the Canadian justice system. The man who killed Greg Pierzchala had been given early release specifically because he was a member of a group that the Government of Canada had defined as "marginalized."

Randall McKenzie's entire adult life had been inflected by charges for violence and illegal firearms. Most recently, he's been handed assault charges for attacking an ex-girlfriend and weapons charges for having an illegal gun on him when he was arrested. McKenzie had been initially denied bail on the grounds that he was too much of a risk to public safety. But only a few months later, an Ontario judge decided that, actually, McKenzie should be free. He was still a violent and unpredictable man. He was still likely to reoffend. He was still a flight risk (he had repeatedly violated court orders in the past).

And as Justice Harrison Arrell openly acknowledged in an audio recording of the bail hearing, it was an "iffy" proposal to release him back into society. But taking precedent over all of these considerations was that McKenzie belonged to a First Nation, the Mississaugas of the Credit First Nation.

"First Nations people are grossly overrepresented in the prison system, especially in pre-trial custody," Arrell would tell Crown prosecutors. While the charges were serious, much was "probably to do with (McKenzie's) native background and education opportunities and employment opportunities and poverty."

The judge would add that his "obligation" in this case was that McKenzie was "a status Aboriginal." It was "something I can't ignore," said Arrell.[3]

McKenzie was released to his mother's house with an ankle bracelet, which he promptly cut off before embarking on a months-long crime spree. At the time McKenzie was accused of killing Pierzchala, he had just crashed a stolen car into a ditch, one of several cars he was accused of stealing since jumping bail.

If Justice Arrell set free a future cop killer entirely on the basis of ethnicity, it was mainly because he was following orders. Starting in 2018, the federal government passed explicit provisions to hand out bail more readily, particularly for Indigenous suspects.

As a guidance document read, judges were now required to consider the "circumstances of Indigenous accused and of accused from vulnerable populations."[4] Almost immediately after the lifting of COVID-19 lockdowns, Canada found itself in the middle of a crime wave unlike anything seen before. The country still hasn't matched the peaks of violent crime charted in the 1990s, but many of the most serious and disturbing crimes have reached all-time highs.

It isn't just that unprecedented numbers of police being killed, but the way it is happening. Historically, Canadian police are killed in the line of duty while chasing down a violent suspect or executing a warrant. Most of the recent police murders have been cold-blooded ambushes.

The "stranger attack," a term that used to barely feature in crime blotters, is now a daily occurrence in Canada's major cities. On a single weekend in 2023, there were two separate incidents of Canadians being randomly stabbed to death in a public place. One, a thirty-seven-year-old man out with his kids at a Vancouver Starbucks,[5] the second a sixteen-year-old boy waiting for a train in a Toronto subway station.[6]

A Leger poll in early 2023 found that not only did the vast majority of respondents feel less safe, but also one in five actually *was* less safe; they directly reported being assaulted, screamed at, or threatened in public.[7] Much of this has been the direct result of a criminal justice system that has explicitly decided that prisons make crime worse, and that the very concept of punishment is a relic. It's also a justice system that has gone all-in on the idea that an offender's identity, rather than their crime, should define how they are punished.

Perhaps unsurprisingly, it didn't take that long for criminals of all stripes to notice that Canada was a place in which they could thrive.

* * *

When Canada's thirteen provincial and territorial premiers sat down for their semi-annual summit in the summer 2024, they represented virtually the entire spectrum of Canadian politics.

The BC NDP premier, David Eby, was a former activist lawyer who had written a book entitled *How to Sue the Police and Private Security in Small Claims Court*. The Alberta premier, Danielle Smith, was a lifelong right-wing populist who was only a few months out from co-hosting a ticketed soiree with former Fox News host Tucker Carlson. But all of these first ministers could agree unanimously on one thing: Canada had to stop releasing criminals all the time. "Police services should not have to chase the same criminal three or four times because of an inadequate bail system," they wrote in a letter to Ottawa. "This not only represents a drain on policing resources but is a hindrance to public safety."

This wasn't the first time they had complained about Canada's so-called "catch and release" justice system. The year before, the thirteen premiers had penned a near-identical letter saying that the Canadian justice system "fundamentally needs to keep anyone who poses a threat to public safety off the streets."

It's a golden rule of criminology that most crime is committed by a startingly small cohort of chronic offenders. And Canada has been actively testing to see how few criminals it takes to throw entire regions into chaos.

In Western Canada, police forces have now begun using the term "superchronic offender," roughly defined as someone who commits more than one crime every month. A 2022 report by the BC Urban Mayors' Caucus detailed how only 204 of these offenders had been responsible for 11,648 negative police contacts within the past year. In Vancouver alone, the city's more prolific forty criminals had racked up 2,152 career convictions between them, an average of fifty-four apiece.[8]

Whole crime waves are now being committed almost entirely by people who just got out of jail or police custody. In the summer 2022, the Vancouver Police started crunching the numbers on the new wave of random, violent assaults plaguing the city. One trend that immediately stood out was that among those arrested for committing a "stranger assault," an incredible 78 percent already had a prior criminal conviction.

In a single three-month period, from March to June 2022, the Vancouver Police arrested forty suspects in connection with stranger attacks. When the "prior police interactions" for all forty suspects were tallied up, the figure came to 3,892, and that was only for police interactions in the Vancouver region.[9]

This is part of why Canadian police departments have become increasingly vocal about the fact that a lot of what they're asked to do doesn't seem to make any sense. As the Canadian Association of Chiefs of Police put it in a 2023 letter, Canada has a "criminal justice system that renders much of our work pointless."[10]

It's a rare day in Canada that goes by without some headline-worthy crime being committed by someone on bail or parole. In BC, the term "catch and release" justice is probably best summed up by the saga of Mohammed Majidpour. In 2022, he attacked a random nineteen-year-old woman in the centre of downtown Vancouver, striking her with a pole while screaming anti-Asian racial slurs. Later that same day, he set fire to a car.

This was not particularly out of character for Majidpour, who had two dozen prior convictions. But after he was eventually tracked down and arrested within a week of the pole attack, he was released on bail after spending just the Thanksgiving weekend in custody. Before October 2022 was finished, Majidpour would be arrested at least two more times. In one instance, he was free just two hours and eighteen minutes before police caught him attempting to steal $330 in leggings from a downtown store. "The officers were familiar with the man, because they'd arrested him the day prior for a different offence," read a police statement.[11]

Consider how lax bail helped to make Canada one of the world's leading centres of auto theft.[12] The problem is so bad that even the justice minister's official car, a government-provided Toyota Highlander, has been stolen three times in three years.[13]

In the summer 2024, Toronto Police announced the breakup of a massive Ontario car theft ring: 124 arrests, 177 stolen vehicles recovered, and 749 charges laid. Of the suspects caught by the dragnet, 44 percent were on bail. And the police didn't even have time to announce the arrests in a press release before 61 percent were given bail.[14]

A few months later, Toronto would produce one of the most iconic images of the Canadian auto theft deluge: a viral doorbell video of a man being struck by his own Porsche Cayenne. The Porsche owner had just handed the keys to a prospective buyer and was walking around the rear of the vehicle when said buyer suddenly jumped in and backed out of the driveway at full speed. The video shows the owner being catapulted into the street before his Cayenne speeds off.

Sarah Badshaw, eighteen, was arrested and handed a slew of charges, including one for "causing bodily harm with a motor vehicle." Nevertheless, she was immediately out on bail. The next day, she was given bail again following charges for a different auto theft.[15]

A lenient justice system is nothing new to Canada. Ever since the 1970s, Canada has been a place in which prisons are viewed almost entirely as rehabilitation centres, and in which even the most heinous crimes can yield shockingly lenient sentences. In 1984, disgruntled Canada Armed Forces corporal Denis Lortie stormed into the Quebec National Assembly with two stolen machine guns, a pistol, and the goal of murdering Quebec Premier Rene Levesque, his cabinet, and any other members of the government he could find. It was only by sheer chance that Lortie entered an empty legislative chamber instead of one packed with hundreds of easy targets. Still, his indiscriminate rampage through the building would kill three and wound thirteen others.

It remains the deadliest act of violence ever committed against a Canadian democratic institution. Lortie was out of jail within eleven years. Convicted on a reduced charge of second-degree murder, he was released on day parole by 1995 and had full parole in time for his thirty-sixth birthday. "I don't think the punishment here fits the crime," Steve Boyer, the son of one of Lortie's victims, told a reporter in 1995.[16]

Punishment is out of vogue in the Canadian prison system. Rather, it is oriented toward the idea that every offender will eventually reenter society, and that its job is to make sure that happens as quickly as possible. That's even the case when it comes to serial killers. Cody Legebokoff was only twenty-four when he was convicted for the murder of three women and a fifteen-year-old girl, Loren Leslie. He had been arrested by an alert RCMP officer shortly after dumping Leslie's body in a remote area. "He lacks any shred of empathy or remorse. He should never be allowed to walk among us again," wrote BC Supreme Court Justice Glen Parrett at Legebokoff's 2014 sentencing.

Only five years later, Legebokoff was moved from a maximum-security prison to a cushier medium-security facility. When the families of his victims reacted with outrage, Corrections Service Canada issued a statement implying that they'd better get used to this, since Legebokoff was eventually getting out. "Rehabilitative efforts, leading to a gradual and controlled release, have proven to be a better way of protecting the public than keeping offenders in maximum security to the end of their sentence, and then releasing them into society without supervision," wrote the agency.[17]

There is no mechanism in Canada under which a convicted felon can be held permanently in jail. Although Canadian media headlines will often speak of a convicted criminal being handed a "life sentence," there's no such thing. The "sentence" doesn't refer to incarceration, only to a parole term that never technically expires.

Ever since Canada formally abolished capital punishment in 1976, the absolute harshest sentence under Canadian law is a guaranteed twenty-two years in prison. Even if a criminal managed to set off an atomic bomb in the center of Montreal, there's no sentence they could be given under which they wouldn't be eligible for full parole after twenty-five years, and early release three years before that.

Public Safety Canada, the agency that oversees the prison system, is always quick to remind critics that "eligibility does not mean automatic release." But in practice, that's how it works. As far back as 2002, an analysis by the Correctional Service of Canada showed that the average first-degree murderer was serving just 22.4 years in prison.[18]

Canadian parole boards are so committed to the doctrine of "reintegrating" offenders that they'll even release convicted child murderers who continue to exhibit a sexual attraction to children. Five-year-old Kimberley Thompson was abducted from the streets of Calgary in 1980 as she walked to kindergarten. She was taken by Harold Smeltzer, a twenty-four-year-old neighbour who by his own account had attacked more than forty women and girls. He had grabbed Kimmie from behind as she stopped to make snowballs and taken her inside his parent's house where he quickly decided to drown her in a bathtub. Smeltzer served just twenty-seven years in prison before he started receiving day parole. He continued to be reupped for parole even after multiple breaches of his release terms and open admissions of feeling attracted to random children he encountered while on release.[19]

* * *

It's also been two decades now that Canada has been experimenting with a justice system that punishes offenders differently based on their race or background. This started in 1995, the year that the government of Prime Minister Jean Chretien amended the Criminal Code to require judges to consider "the circumstances of aboriginal offenders" before handing down a sentence.

The idea of the reform was to address Indigenous "overrepresentation" in prison. In one stark example, by the late 1980s the inmates in Saskatchewan prisons were 60 percent Indigenous, despite representing only 7 percent of the provincial population.

The policy of race-differentiated sentencing was ultimately codified in the 1999 Supreme Court decision R v. Gladue. Jamie Tanis Gladue, nineteen, had stabbed her common-law husband to death in a drunken rage, accusing him of having an affair with her older sister. She was convicted of manslaughter, and her sentence of three years imprisonment was appealed all the way to Canada's highest court to see if it truly jibed with the new rules regarding Gladue's "circumstances" as a Cree woman. The Supreme Court not only said it did but also enshrined the adoption of so-called "Gladue reports." Ever since, whenever an Indigenous offender is facing sentencing, the judge has to first read through a commissioned report listing the "systemic or background factors" that may have influenced the crime. "The jail term for an aboriginal offender may in some circumstances be less than the term imposed on a non-aboriginal offender for the same offence," reads the Gladue decision.

Gladue reports have now been the law of the land for nearly twenty-five years, but it's particularly in the last ten years that identity-based justice and an institutional distaste for punishment have combined into an unholy regime in which seemingly nobody goes to jail.

Anti-racism doctrine has been embraced by the Canadian justice system harder than almost anywhere else. In 2021, the Department of Justice openly declared that it was shot through with systemic racism that had resulted in the "over-incarceration of Indigenous peoples, Black Canadians, and members of marginalized communities." "Rooting out systemic racism is key to a fair and effective justice system," it said.[20]

One result of this declaration was a proposal to loosen the punishments for gun criminals, even as Ottawa was simultaneously leading a drive to crack down on gun crime by banning whole categories of firearms. In December 2021, the Department of Justice proposed stripping the minimum prison sentences from eleven gun crimes, including "robbery with a firearm," "extortion with a firearm," and "discharging firearm with intent." The reasoning was that non-white Canadians were disproportionately convicted of these crimes, which made them racist. "Sentencing laws that have focused on punishment through imprisonment have disproportionately affected Indigenous peoples, as well as Black Canadians and members of marginalized communities," read a backgrounder.[21]

And this was despite the fact that Canada didn't really have an over-incarceration problem, at least not in the way that the term was used in American anti-racism literature. The term was often employed in the United States, and it made much more sense in a country home to the world's largest population of incarcerated prisoners (about 1.8 million as of the last count).[22] But the Canadian prison population is almost the exact opposite: The nonprofit World Prison Brief is the usual authority on prison populations, and it has long pegged Canada as having the lowest incarceration rate in the Western Hemisphere. According to its 2015 count, the United States was locking up prisoners at a rate seven times that of Canada.

Canada's prison population was more in league with Spain, Belgium, Portugal, and Luxembourg, all of which have dramatically lower rates of violent crime.[23]

Additionally, the Parole Board of Canada declared itself an agent of "systemic discrimination." In a forty-five-page "diversity, equity and inclusion" report published in 2022, the board said that high number of Black people in Canadian prisons was due entirely to "systemic oppression, marginalization, and disenfranchisement that is so deeply entrenched in Canadian society that it is functionally normalized."[24]

It followed that when board members were weighing whether to release a criminal from prison, they were to consider the offender was in jail simply because the "discrimination and marginalization of Black people" had driven them to a life of crime. "Underlying social and economic factors contribute to criminalization and it is important to address systemic inequality in all areas of society in order to make meaningful change toward substantive equity."

Now, whenever an offender is being sentenced or considered for parole, it's not uncommon that the hearing will spend far more time parsing over the details of the offender's childhood and family history rather than the crime committed.

In 2024, a BC man, Anthony Woods, was being sentenced for a fatal stabbing he had committed at a Vancouver transitional housing facility. Four years prior, Woods had been causing a scene at the facility, yelling and pounding on doors. When a seventy-two-year-old visitor, Alex Gortmaker, apparently confronted Woods about the ruckus, he received a stab wound in reply. Woods produced a knife, stabbed Gortmaker in the chest, and pushed him to the ground where he bled to death.

The sentencing decision went into granular detail about Woods' life. His mother's drug problem. His time in foster care. His ADHD diagnosis. The Indian residential schools were attended by Woods' grandparents and extended family. The generalized impact of Canada's "colonial history and post-colonial assimilationist policies." The decision even detailed how he spent his summers growing up. "Mr. Woods recalls playing with cousins, picking berries and learning how to cut and jar fish," it read.

His victim got a single cursory section, 200 words out of the 8,000-word decision.

Gortmaker's niece Sandra was brought in to read a victim impact statement saying, "she is haunted with nightmares; that going outside fills her with anxiety; that her foundation of trust and empathy has been lost; and that words do not properly capture the depth of her sorrow."

Ultimately, a judge ruled that the "fair, fit and principled sentence" for Woods was to release him immediately. He ultimately served just eight months of pre-trial detention for the crime.

The Canadian justice system's obsession with identity has also made Canada likely the only country on earth, which holds that citizens should be treated harsher by the courts than noncitizens. According to a 2014 Supreme Court decision, foreigners convicted of crimes should have "collateral consequences" factored into their sentencing. In other words, if the conviction is likely to get the offender deported, that should count as part of their punishment.

In 2024, an Alberta judge cited this exact precedent in refusing to convict a twenty-five-year-old foreign student found guilty of sexual assault for groping an eighteen-year-old at a nightclub. If he was Canadian, he probably would have gotten at least a criminal record. Instead, the conviction was discharged in "consideration of the devastating collateral immigration consequences to recording a conviction."[25]

* * *

If crime in Canada has truly taken a turn into the ridiculous in recent years, much of the blame can be placed on a single piece of legislation that took all of Canada's various experiments in identity-based justice and supercharged them. Bill C-75, which entered into law in the summer of 2019, was the Trudeau government's signature crime reform bill. Designed to "modernize the criminal justice system," the bill notably included a series of provisions making it much easier for accused criminals to obtain bail.

The bill's creators were quite open about the fact that easier bail was the goal. In introducing C-75 to the House of Commons, then Justice Minister Jody Wilson-Raybould criticized Canada's prior bail system for perpetuating a "cycle of incarceration" and for disproportionately impacting "Indigenous people and marginalized Canadians."

Henceforth, judges would be ordered to grant bail "at the earliest possible opportunity" and to spend much more time considering the ethnicity of the bail seeker before them. As per the bill's text, bail would need to be granted more readily to anyone who belonged to "a vulnerable population that is over-represented in the criminal justice system."

The bill didn't even like the idea of bail conditions. That is, releasing a suspect on bail but requiring them to avoid certain neighbourhoods, stick to a curfew, or avoid alcohol. C-75 mandated that all this bail should be handed out under the "least onerous conditions."

Pretty much immediately, the effect of Bill C-75 was to ensure that basically everyone got bail and continued to receive bail even if they violated their conditions or were charged with additional crimes. At one point in 2023, the BC Prosecution Service took the unusual step of publishing data to show just how rare it was for violent suspects to get their bail revoked.[26] Over a five-week period, the BC Prosecution Service counted 425 bail hearings involving a suspect who had been charged with a violent crime while already on bail for a prior offence. In 327 of those hearings (76 percent), the suspect was simply given bail again.

In 2022, British Columbia's Justice Minister was veteran environmental lawyer Murray Rankin. He was part of a provincial government not particularly known for being "tough on crime." Among other things, the government had championed the decriminalization of illicit drugs and the distribution of government-supplied "safer supply" opioids. Rankin had also been a federal MP when C-75 was passed, where his main critique of the reform was that it didn't go far enough.[27] But as his province became seized by a crisis of stranger attacks committed by the same few hundred chronic offenders, Rankin was put into the strange position of publicly advocating for the federal government to start keeping people in jail for longer.

As Rankin told reporters at the time, Bill C-75 had yielded "unintended consequences."[28]

One of the consequences of a justice system based on immutable characteristics is that it pretty quickly yielded a whole cottage industry of criminals pretending to be part of a marginalized group in order to evade punishment. When BC man Nathan Legault was convicted for a raft of child sexual assault crimes committed while he was working as a pastor, he was about to face sentencing when he suddenly mentioned that one of his great-great-grandparents was a member Haudenosaunee Confederacy and that he was, therefore, entitled to a Gladue review.

A sentencing judge drafted a decision going into granular detail about Legault's tenuous Indigenous links before concluding that it had no bearing on his eventual "child pornography addiction." That same decision would warn other judges to gird themselves for a flood of similar attempts at "Indigenous identity fraud."

"A Tsunami is coming; driven by the desire of non-Indigenous people to get what they perceive to be the benefits of identifying as Indigenous," it read.[29]

One of the alternative sentencing options that arose in the wake of the Gladue decision was a new network of Indigenous "healing lodges"—low-security rehabilitation centres that could serve as an alternative to hard time in a federal prison. In 2018, it emerged that Terri-Lynne McClintic, one of Canada's most notorious child murderers, had secured transfer to a Saskatchewan healing lodge despite no Indigenous background whatsoever. The transfer was particularly surprising to the Nekaneet First Nation, the Saskatchewan band on whose land the healing lodge was located. The lodge had opened in 1995 as a way to get Indigenous female offenders back on the straight and narrow. But with the federal government having nixed any Nekaneet role in inmate selection, it wasn't until the McClintic transfer made headlines that members realized that a woman who had abducted and murdered a nine-year-old with a hammer was now housed just a short walk from the Nekaneet School. "I believe if our elders were still a part of the process maybe Ms. McClintic wouldn't be at the healing lodge," Nekaneet Chief Alvin Francis said at the time.[30]

Along the way, legal scholars were noticing that none of this seemed to be working as intended. "Over representation," the siren call of Canada's move to stratify the justice system along racial lines, remains as high as ever. In 2008, 20 percent of federal inmate were Indigenous. Ten years later, it was 28 percent.[31]

An internal Department of Justice report noted this trend in 2017, but generally concluded that the solution was to focus even harder on the identity of offenders: Gladue reports should start including gender analysis and more granular details such as whether an accused's "grandparents were residential school survivors." It continued: "Gladue should not be regarded as a panacea for overrepresentation, but rather as a contribution to the efforts required."[32]

As Canada has leaned ever harder into its catch-and-release odyssey, it's often found itself directly at odds with First Nations governments openly campaigning for more policing and harsher sentencing for repeat offenders, regardless of ethnicity. And the reason is simple: while Canada's criminals are disproportionately Indigenous, so are their victims.

Winnipeg Police Chief Danny Smyth would say as much during an August 2023 summit on bail policy. "What I think people sometimes overlook is that the victims of crime are the very communities that (we're) talking about," said Smyth, who was then the serving president of the Canadian Association of Chiefs of Police.[33]

In 2022, the James Smith Cree Nation in Saskatchewan was subjected to a horrifying mass stabbing in which an attacker went door-to-door, slashing whole families and ultimately killing eleven. The attacker was a familiar figure by Canadian justice standards. Myles Sanderson had fifty-nine criminal convictions and a history of explosive, random violence. But none of that had prevented Sanderson from obtaining early release from prison the year before, where he'd been serving a sentence for assault.[34] Sanderson then violated his release conditions and dropped off the radar before emerging a few months later as Canada's newest spree killer.

When the Assembly of First Nations convened a national justice forum in 2022, "overrepresentation" was indeed a top agenda item, but the solution was deemed to be greater local control of policing and justice, rather than the "sentencing circles and Gladue reports" mandated by Ottawa.[35]

"One of the complaints I've heard, particularly from Indigenous women is how, unfortunately, it's been men in positions of power when there's been sexual assault or some wrongdoing, in the sense that they will use restorative justice to have an easier sentence. And I don't know what the solution is, but this is something that needs to be researched," said one participant.

What the Canadian legal system has done over the past generation is to become laser-focused on the notion that past traumas and current inequities can be solved simply by tweaking the numbers, and that jail or policing isn't a reaction to society's problems, but the cause of them. But in so doing, Canada has proved remarkably disdainful to those same marginalized communities whenever they ask the courts to at least stop handing them new traumas.

When convicted murderer Kenneth MacKay was granted day parole just twenty-three years after brutally murdering twenty-one-year-old Indigenous woman Crystal Paskemin, it was the Federation of Sovereign Indigenous Nations who said that a proper country would have sentenced him to die in jail. "Kenneth MacKay has violated the basic principles of human dignity and justice, and he has forfeited his right to belong to a civilized community," it wrote in a 2023 statement.[36]

The year before, when Winnipeg man Jeremy Skibicki was arrested for the serial murders of four Indigenous women, one of the first reactions of Manitoba First Nations leaders was to note the "cruel joke" that he would probably make parole one day.

"We are faced with the grim reality that murderers, even those who have taken the life of a child, can be given as little as five years in prison," David Monias, chief of the Pimicikamak Cree Nation, told the Aboriginal Peoples Television Network. "These individuals are then released back into our communities, free to walk amongst us as if they haven't destroyed lives."[37]

8 | The World's Most Expensive Free Health Care

In September 2009, a woman in the waiting room of Winnipeg's Health Sciences Centre noticed that a man near her was no longer breathing.

"I think that man over there in the wheelchair is dead," she said to the security guard, Gary Francis.

To Francis, the man looked like he was sleeping, but a simple pinch of his neck revealed that he was dead, and had been for quite some time. When the guard quietly wheeled the man into a rear area, medical staff initially scoffed at the notion that the slumped figure before them was a corpse.

"I said 'I need some help here, I think the fellow here is dead.' They thought I was joking," Francis would later testify.[1]

Brian Sinclair, a forty-five-year-old double amputee, had gone to the hospital complaining of abdominal pains due to a blocked catheter. All he needed was a routine ninety-minute procedure and a prescription of antibiotics, and he'd be on his way.

Instead, after checking in at a reception desk, Sinclair was abandoned for thirty-four hours.

His prolonged death throes included three separate instances of vomiting, all of which were cleaned up by janitorial staff without any nurse being summoned to check Sinclair's condition. At one point, a security guard alerted medical staff to Sinclair's curiously long stay in the waiting room and was told that he'd already been treated and was now sleeping.

A cascade of failures contributed to Sinclair's demise. An emergency department that was busier than usual. A nursing department that was short-staffed. And multiple instances of hospital workers assuming that Sinclair was a sleeping homeless man, rather than a forgotten patient going into shock. If just one element had been different, Sinclair would have survived.

The failure was so egregious, so unprecedented, that many within the medical community argued that Sinclair, who was Indigenous, had ultimately died of prejudice more than any specific medical failure.

But it was a social and political scandal that would resonate for years. The name "Brian Sinclair" would appear thousands of times in Canadian media over the next decade, as would the phrase "ignored to death." His demise would spawn a lengthy judicial inquest, a full-scale review of the provincial health system,[2] a criminal investigation, and calls for the resignation of Manitoba's minister of health.

Ten years after Sinclair's death, a cousin named Robert Sinclair described going to the Winnipeg Health Sciences Centre following a chainsaw accident and being met at the door by a medical team. "They probably didn't want another Sinclair dying in their hospital," he would tell the Canadian Press.[3]

Yet, nowadays, Canadians are ignored to death in hospital waiting rooms all the time. A woman died in a North Vancouver waiting room after spending two days on a stretcher. Witnesses would report that she was strenuously polite and understanding right to the end.[4]

A sixty-seven-year-old Cape Breton woman gave up and went home after waiting seven hours for care to address mysterious flu-like symptoms. Shortly after returning home, she died.[5]

And as waiting room deaths become a matter of routine, the official responses have been wholly different.

Brian Sinclair's death was seen as a preventable tragedy by a health system that could have kept him safe if it had been working properly. But these new patients aren't dying because someone screwed up. They are the expected casualties of a health system where deadly overcrowding is now the norm.

In the case of the North Vancouver death, a nurse told local media that they simply did not have enough staff to stop the woman from dying. "The moral distress of that waiting room, the list of things that you could not do, is gut-wrenching," she said.[6]

Late in 2023, Montreal's Anna-Laberge Hospital confirmed that two people had died in its waiting room in a matter of days. Quebec's official association for emergency medicine specialists told local media that the deaths were a "nightmare," but the consequence of a hospital that had been operating at 200 percent capacity for six consecutive weeks.

"You basically put patients anywhere they will fit, computer systems have problems keeping track of those patients, the ratio of nurses-per-patient explodes, and it becomes to the point where triage nurse is basically the worst job in the hospital because the waiting room is full and nobody gets seen and then bad things happen to patients," said Gilbert Boucher, president of Association des spécialistes en médecine d'urgence du Québec.[7]

In some rural areas, even the prospect of dying in a waiting room is becoming a luxury. Starting in 2022, hospitals being forced into temporary shutdowns due to staff shortages became a nationwide phenomenon. In the first months of 2024, the BC city of Merritt, population 7,000, saw its only hospital plunged into sudden day-long closures roughly every couple of weeks.[8] Anybody showing up to the ER would be met with a sign telling them to drive 90 kilometres to Kamloops or to try calling the fire department.

Ashcroft, BC, population 1,600, saw a woman die of a heart attack despite living within sight of the local hospital. Its ER department was closed for the night, and the community's single ambulance was busy with another call.[9]

Canadian health care has long been characterized by shortages and wait times, both of which were symptoms of a problem that lay at the core of how the system is organized. Canada mandates a uniquely inflexible form of socialized medicine that is unlike any other in the world, with the gradual result that Canadians were getting less bang for their health care dollar than almost anyone else.

The traditional way to dismiss this was to note that, whatever its faults, at least Canadian health care is free. But in just the last few years, the shortages have been so overwhelming that the maxim isn't working anymore. Americans might have to pay for their doctor, but at least they have a doctor.

To a Canadian, the nightmare US scenario is one in which an uninsured American suddenly finds themselves in need of medical attention and is slapped with a financially devastating bill as a result. It's the premise of *Breaking Bad*, the AMC miniseries in which a high school teacher turns to cooking meth in order to cover his cancer bills. "Canadian *Breaking Bad*" became an internet trope; protagonist Walter White would be given his cancer diagnosis, a benevolent medicare system would immediately begin free-of-charge chemotherapy treatments, and the series would be over.

In reality, the Canadian equivalent to *Breaking Bad* is increasingly becoming one in which Walter White dies on a waiting list. That is, if he ever gets the diagnosis at all.

In 2022, a couple in Victoria, BC placed a page two ad in the local daily newspaper declaring "Wanted: Licensed medical doctor for prescription renewal. Urgent! Please?"[10]

The ad concerned eighty-two-year-old Michael Mort. After Mort's doctor had retired, he had joined the nearly one million British Columbians without a family doctor and with minimal prospect of finding one. The city's walk-in clinics were now permanently booked to capacity. Even telehealth was a lost cause. As the ad explained, there were "no virtual appointments available for months."

As Mort's wife Janet would tell the *Victoria Times Colonist*, she had placed the ad in panic after watching her husband visibly deteriorate due entirely to an inability to get new meds prescribed. "I cried myself to sleep feeling there was nothing left that I could do," she said.

If you're comparing health care systems based purely on how many people are dying because of an inability to access care, of late the US system has been doing exponentially better than Canada. An oft-cited statistic is that 45,000 Americans die each year due to a lack of health insurance. That comes from a 2009 estimate published in the *American Journal of Public Health*.[11] A 2023 analysis of Canadian data found that 17,032 patients died in a single year while waiting for surgery or a diagnostic scan. And that estimate was based on incomplete data; the total number of fatalities could have been as high as 31,000, according to SecondStreet.org, which did the analysis.[12]

Given that the Canadian population is only about a tenth of the United States, this would suggest that Canada has at least five times more people dying because they don't have proper health care.

One of the most brazen official admissions as to the superiority of the US health system came in May 2023. That was the month the BC Ministry of Health announced that its waiting list for radiation treatment had become so critical that it was going to start outsourcing treatment to clinics in Washington State. The ministry knew how bad this looked, but officials explained that lives were legitimately on the line. "Timely radiation therapy treatment is critical for people with cancer, both for their survival and overall quality of life," explained Dr. Kim Chi, BC's top cancer doctor.[13]

But it's against Canada's peers in the rest of the developed world, all of whom similarly maintain systems of socialized medicine, that the Canadian health system truly emerges as a catastrophic outlier. According to data from the Organisation for Economic Co-operation and Development (OECD), a club comprising the world's thirty-eight most developed nations, Canada trails the first world in hospital beds per capita.

In 2020, Canada was fifth from the bottom with just 2.5 beds per 1,000 inhabitants (about one hospital bed for every 400 Canadians).[14] Compare that to France, with one bed for every 166 citizens. Or Japan and South Korea, who topped the list with one for every 80 people.

The figures are even worse when it comes to acute care beds. In 2017, Canada was in last place in the OECD ranking of acute care bed ratios.[15] Canada had two ICU beds per 1000 inhabitants, as compared to seven for South Korea, the top-ranked country.

This was thrown into stark relief during the COVID-19 pandemic when even mild upticks in COVID-19 infections were enough to throw Canadian hospitals into crisis. COVID-19 waves that could have been easily absorbed by a more functional healthcare system repeatedly resulted in draconian government strictures and lockdowns to keep emergency rooms from being overwhelmed.

As far back as 2016, the Commonwealth Fund, a health-care think tank headquartered in New York, did a comparison of health systems in the world's eleven wealthiest nations and found that Canadians experienced some of the longest health care wait times of any of them.[16]

If an Australian needed something looked at, the Commonwealth Fund found that 69 percent of them could expect to see a doctor either that day or the next. In the United Kingdom, it was 59 percent. In Canada, the idea of a "same or next-day appointment" was out of reach for most patients, the worst ranking of any country looked at.[17] The same was true of specialist appointments: 30 percent of Canadians could expect a wait of at least two months to see a specialist compared to just 3 percent in Germany or 4 percent in France.

None of this is for lack of resources. According to 2024 data compiled by the Canadian Institute for Health Information, health expenditures in Canada are now $9,054 per person, per year, among the highest in the OECD.[18] In 2022, the average OECD nation was spending the equivalent of $6,300 per person.

To put it another way, if every Canadian was given $9,000 per year to spend on private health insurance, they could likely afford an American plan offering levels of health care access beyond their wildest dreams. For a family of five, that's $45,000 worth of health insurance per year, nearly fifty percent more than the USD$23,968 (about $34,000) that it costs for an average family plan in the United States as of 2023.[19]

The Commonwealth Fund has noted this phenomenon as well. Another regular survey of theirs ranks first-world health care systems based on the bang they're getting for their health buck. In 2021, they ranked the world's eleven wealthiest countries on "health care system performance compared to spending." The Americans were at the bottom. Canada was conspicuously in second-to-last place, the worst of any other country with a universal system.[20]

The Canada-based Fraser Institute has found much the same thing. In a 2019 report that ranked the "value for money" of twenty-eight universal healthcare systems around the world, Canada stood out for spending the most to get the least. Only Switzerland was found to be spending more of its GDP on health care, and it was getting top-tier access. Canada, by contrast, was lagging on everything from wait times to the number of MRI machines in operation. "Although Canada's is among the most expensive universal-access health-care systems in the OECD, its performance is modest to poor," concluded the report.[21]

Most Canadians remain in the dark as to these international disparities. They're probably even less aware that their government operates a more extreme version of public health care than elsewhere in the free world.

The usual strategy is to enshrine a free "public option" that covers the basics and to leave everything else in the hands of a private system. If you're having a baby in Australia, you can book a shared room at a public hospital, or if you've got private insurance, you can opt for a cush room in a private hospital complete with a dedicated obstetrician.

The United Kingdom's famed National Health System is so comprehensive that it offers prescription eyeglasses. But for the equivalent of between $1,000 and $3000 per year, a Brit can obtain insurance to access the country's network of private hospitals. Private health insurance "gives you a choice in the level of care you get, and how and when it's provided," reads an official UK government guide.[22] It adds that "you can use your insurance to reduce the time you spend waiting for NHS treatment, if your wait time is more than six weeks."

In Canada, all of these options are illegal. If a procedure is offered by the government, it is forbidden to have that same procedure covered by private insurance. Or, as a Government of Canada explainer puts it, "private health insurance plans are prohibited from duplicating coverage for health services provided in Canada which are insured under the Canada Health Act."[23]

Private clinics are allowed to provide covered procedures, but the bill has to be paid in cash.

Virtually no other country does this. Everywhere in Europe, from Brussels to Oslo, a public system is paired with a private system available to anyone willing to purchase extra coverage. Even in the People's Republic of China, the world's largest communist country, you can either get in line with the public system, or for about $5,000 in annual insurance premiums gain access to the country's system of private hospitals.[24]

The closest analogue to the Canadian system would be Cuba. Private health care, as with every other aspect of the private sector in Cuba, is banned.

One of the consequences of maintaining such strict governmental controls on health care is that it's led to a situation where Canada artificially limits the supply of doctors who can be trained each year. Canada has seventeen publicly funded medical schools, and they're actively prevented from training more than about 3,000 new doctors per year.[25]

This would be inconceivable for any other profession. There are no state-mandated limits on the number of auto mechanics, dentists, or veterinarians being trained each year. But all of those professions are mostly expected to draw their pay from private sources; if they can't find a job, it's on them. Since Canada assumes that every new doctor will be drawing a government paycheque, it permits schools only to train the number of doctors it figures it can afford. In 2018, for example, the budget-conscious Quebec health minister decided the province was churning out too many graduates and cut the number of permitted medical school admissions.[26] Unsurprisingly, all these quotas in med schools have led to Canada's noticeable shortage of family doctors.

The Commonwealth Fund certainly noticed. When lining up Canada against its peer countries in terms of access to "primary care," it found that Canada had fallen to last place. In 2023, just 86 percent of Canadians reported "having a doctor or a place they usually go for medical care." That may sound high, but it stood at a respectable 93 percent just seven years prior. Despite Canada's claim to universal health care, it now means that one in every seven Canadians (14 percent) has to camp out in a hospital emergency room if they need so much as a prescription. Given current trends, it may only be another two or three years until this situation describes 10 million Canadians.[27] That's equivalent to the entire population of Western Canada not having a family doctor.

The Canadian governmental stranglehold on who's allowed to deliver health care has also yielded a system whose purview keeps getting bigger and more elaborate, even as its ability to deliver gets worse. Every passing year, as waitlists get longer and emergency rooms more backed up, increasing numbers of procedures fall under the "medically necessary" umbrella of the Canada Health Act. A more flexible system could simply resolve to provide the basics as efficiently and equitably as possible and leave the more elaborate surgeries to private insurers. That's essentially how Canada runs its school system: the public schools will teach you math, science, and the 100-metre dash, but if you want a top-tier theatre arts program or sailing curriculum, you'll probably have to find the tuition for a private school.

In Canada, if a medical procedure exists, the seventy-year-old doctrine of Canadian Medicare holds that the government should rightly be the one to perform it. The system's capacity to cover all these procedures without overextending itself is irrelevant.

One of the more extreme examples of this came in 2024 when an Ontario court ordered the province's public health insurer to cover the costs of a "penile preserving vaginoplasty." The Ontario Health Insurance Plan already covered vaginoplasties and penosplasties: the two so-called transgender "bottom surgeries." But this procedure was something different: a surgery to create an artificial vaginal canal in addition to keeping the penis. The applicant, known in court documents only as K.S., identified as non-binary and wanted a vagina without losing the ability to orgasm or urinate properly. Only one clinic in Texas was known to offer the "penile preserving vaginoplasty" surgery. K.S.'s lawyers argued that if the Canadian health system didn't front the US$10,000 to $70,000 for the procedure and instead forced K.S. to undergo a conventional vaginoplasty, it was guilty of a kind of "conversion therapy."[28] In a unanimous decision, the Ontario Divisional Court not only agreed but also ruled that it was a charter right for K.S. to have a vagina and penis at the same time. Requiring K.S. "to remove their penis to receive state funding for a vaginoplasty would be inconsistent with the values of equality and security of the person."

It didn't escape notice that the Canadian government started covering penile-preserving vaginoplasties at the exact same time when Canadians were being approved for assisted suicide for no other reason than they couldn't secure proper health care.

In 2022, the Canadian fashion retailer Simons made the odd marketing decision to release a three-minute commercial documenting a thirty-seven-year-old woman's last days on earth before her scheduled MAID appointment.

Simons took the ad down from its website after it emerged that its subject, Jennifer Hatch, would have preferred to live but gave up after years of unsuccessfully seeking care for a painful genetic condition. As Hatch had told a CTV interviewer before her death, "I feel like I'm falling through the cracks so if I'm not able to access health care, am I then able to access death care?"[29]

A particularly horrifying twist on the standard Canadian story of a patient dying in a hospital waiting room came only a few weeks after the K.S. decision. In early 2024, quadriplegic Normand Meunier, sixty-six, went to the hospital for a respiratory virus and ended up waiting four days on a stretcher that gave him a bedsore so severe that it exposed bone. Rather than undergo the months-long process to heal the sore, he opted to be euthanized.[30]

* * *

As with many crises described in this book, the Canadian health care system has been able to achieve its abject collapse thanks, in large part, to a national conviction that everything is fine. Because the Canadian health system isn't just a health system; for many, it defines their understanding of what it means to be Canadian.

In a 2023 Canada Day survey, the "health care system" topped the rankings as the one thing that respondents were most proud of: 74 percent expressed pride in Canadian Medicare, as compared to 65 percent who got a warm, patriotic feeling from Canada's "scientific technological achievements."[31]

When CBC commissioned a thirteen-episode 2004 miniseries designed to find the "greatest Canadian," the winner was Tommy Douglas, the populist Saskatchewan politician typically credited as the "father of Medicare."

Over the last decade the phrase "best health care system in the world" has been unironically uttered more than a dozen times in the House of Commons by representatives of all the major parties.

In April 2024, Health Minister Mark Holland defended the need for pharmacare by saying it would ensure "Canadians have access to the greatest health care system in the world."

From the Conservative opposition benches, Alberta's Matt Jeneroux declared in 2020 that Canada didn't need pharmacare because "we already have one of the best health care systems in the world."

At the height of Arcade Fire's fame in 2016, the Montreal indie band easily ranked as one of the world's most visible Canadian institutions. It used its platform to lecture Americans about the superiority of the Canadian system. When Arcade Fire frontman Win Butler was awarded Most Valuable Player after an NBA Celebrity All-Star game, he celebrated by declaring into an ESPN microphone "the US has a lot they can learn from Canada: health care, taking care of people."[32]

But with each closed emergency room and waiting room death, that faith gets more difficult to sustain. Polls now show a populace embracing ideas that would have been unthinkable only a few years ago.

An Ipsos poll in 2023 found that 60 percent of Canadians now favoured private health care for those who can afford it. Darrell Bricker, CEO of Ipsos Public Affairs, told a Global News interviewer that in his thirty years as a pollster, he's never seen "a majority of Canadians saying they're open to considering private methods of delivery."[33]

An Angus Reid Institute survey from that same year was particularly illuminating. When respondents were asked if they supported more "private delivery of care," 49 percent reflexively said "no." But after the respondents were told about the functional private care systems operating in Germany and the United Kingdom, seven percent changed their mind on the spot.[34]

Probably the most telling indicator of Canadians' shifting views on their health system is that millions no longer believe that if their health takes a turn, the "best health care system in the world" will be waiting to bail them out. In 2018, the pollster Research Co. found that 77 percent of respondents were confident that if they got sick or had an accident, they'd be able to get the care they needed.[35] A mere eighteen months later, after COVID-19 had exposed some of the worst deficiencies of the Canadian system, that figure had dropped to 67 percent, a 10-point plunge. Stratified out across the entire Canadian population, that's the equivalent of about four million people suddenly deciding that if they find a lump one morning, they're probably on their own.

It's yielding a Canada more likely to accept pragmatic changes to a system whose failures have so often been concealed by mythos and jingoism. But it did take an ungodly tithe of death and carnage to get there.

Conclusion

Also, the Economy Sucks

And on top of everything else, the economy sucks.

Arguably the most important economic indicator, Gross Domestic Product per capita, is in freefall in Canada. Each passing year, the average Canadian earns less money and can afford fewer things compared to the rest of the developed world. Canada "has lagged behind the US and other advanced economies in terms of standard of living," warned a TD Bank report from July 2023. "What's more, little turnaround appears to be on the horizon."[1]

And it's a long horizon. In 2021 the OECD did some calculations on how its member states were set to perform over the next forty years. Canada ranked in last place. By 2060, Canada is expected to be the world's worst performing advanced economy.[2]

The decline has been most notable when compared to the United States. For much of the twentieth century, Canada and the United States enjoyed similar rates of economic growth. As recently as 2014, US economists were arguing that Canada was actually a better steward of the American Dream than America itself. At the time, Canada's income growth was more broadly shared than in the United States, and it also had better economic mobility: a Canadian born into poverty was far more likely to become a millionaire than their US equivalent.[3]

But 2014 was also the year everything started to fall apart. It was the year that Saudi Arabia started over-drilling in a bid to crater oil prices and drive other petro-nations out of business. The United States recovered pretty quickly from the oil price shock, and Canada very conspicuously did not. It let productivity and capital investment slide and all but abandoned its resource sector.

The government of Justin Trudeau, elected in 2015, didn't singularly cause the decline, but it certainly took prosperity for granted. Canada has effectively spent the last decade under a government that never really concerned itself with economic growth. This is something highlighted often by former Bank of Canada Governor David Dodge. Since at least 2021, every time the Trudeau government releases a budget, Dodge can usually be relied upon to say that it doesn't look like the work of people who want a wealthier and more productive Canada. "We're going in exactly the wrong direction," Dodge said of the 2024 budget.[4]

According to Statistics Canada, if Canada had simply kept up with the Americans and maintained its 2015 growth rates, every Canadian would be earning an extra $4,200 per year by now.[5]

One of the hardest pills to swallow has been the simple fact that Canada is no longer among the world's richest nations.[6] At the end of the Cold War, the wealth of the average Canadian was bested only by Switzerland, Luxembourg, the United States, and the richer corners of Scandinavia.

Now, Canada isn't even in the top ten. One by one, everyone from Ireland to Iceland to Australia has pulled ahead.

This means that just as Canadians are noticing males in the women's change room or seeing that their downtowns are filled with discarded syringes and random stabbings, they're also realizing that they're poor.

* * *

If I can sum up over what went wrong with Canada over the past decade or so, it's that the country decided to run absolutely everything on the honour system and didn't have the imagination to consider why this would be a bad idea.

Legislators encoded "gender identity" protections into law without considering that it would be employed by shop teachers to show up to work in fetish gear.

Criminologists recommended a kinder, gentler approach to bail, without wondering how they would deal with the criminals who simply decided to ignore their release conditions.

The Supreme Court assumed that Canada could handle a low-barrier approach to assisted suicide and was surprised when libertine doctors took this as a license to start euthanizing the poor and vulnerable.

Communities trusted that the managers put in charge of a new safe injection site were serious when they said they wanted to get drug users into treatment.

More than almost any other nation, Canadians trusted their leaders not to turn the country into a petri dish for bad ideas. And ironically, this is a big reason why the bad ideas were able to become so entrenched, so quickly.

There were vanishingly few safeguards in place, and many Canadians lacked the imagination to conceive that their system was capable of such dysfunction. A national faith that "this can't be happening in Canada" ended up yielding a whole bunch of ghastly scenarios that were *only* happening in Canada.

One easy explanation for this naivety is that until quite recently Canada has generally worked well. The Canadian "points-based" immigration system was considered among the world's best. Canada had effectively invented the idea of an immigration system based on merit rather than ethnicity or place of origin: starting in the 1960s, anyone who spoke the language and had an applicable skill had a chance of getting in. The eventual result was one of the most ethnically heterogeneous countries on earth, as well as one that was almost entirely devoid of nativist, anti-immigration sentiment. For a time, the Conservative Party of Canada was effectively the only right-wing party on earth that saw high immigration as a net benefit to the country. By opening up Canadian immigration to wildly unsustainable highs starting in 2022, the federal betrayed Canada's sixty-year streak of integrating newcomers better than anyone else.

Whatever systemic problems existed in health care or the Canadian justice system were largely invisible to the average citizen. Nobody was dying in hospital waiting rooms and "stranger attacks" weren't a common occurrence. In fact, from 1995 straight through to 2015, crime experienced a steady decline. In 2014, Canada posted a murder rate lower than at any point since the mid-1960s.

Roll it all together, and Canadians had become a people who were unusually confident that their institutions knew what they were doing. Although Jordan Peterson has since become a vociferous critic of Canada's various failings (he officially moved to the United States in late 2024), his first round of viral YouTube videos in 2014 actually lamented how strange it was that his country would do something as irrational as mandating preferred pronouns. "I would say to some very large degree that Canada has been reasonably free of this," he said.[7]

Public trust has long been weirdly high in Canada. The OECD conducts regular surveys of public trust across its member states, and Canada always scores well above average. The latest survey, published in 2023, shows 49 percent of Canadians placing "high or moderately high" trust in their national government.[8] This is a higher level of public trust than any European country, save Luxembourg and Switzerland. It is higher than any single country in Scandinavia, the usual analogue for competent, low-corruption governments. Norwegians, Swedes, Finns, and Danes all like their political systems, but not quite with the same loyalty as a Canadian.

Canadians, unfortunately, have put all that trust in a system with remarkably few checks on power. The average American president has to wade through a thicket of Senate approvals and Congressional compromises to push through an agenda. The typical European leader commands a shaky coalition government. But the prime minister of Canada retains a level of executive power that is utterly mind-blowing by the standards of his peers in the rest of the G7.

The prime minister retains exclusive control over the appointment of senators and judges. He even appoints his own boss, the governor-general, when the position becomes vacant. And that power swells even more if the prime minister is in charge of a majority government. Caucus dissent is extremely rare in Canada, meaning that even an unpopular prime minister has little to stop them from continuing to push through a legislative agenda. Way back in 2001, the political journalist Jeffrey Simpson wrote in *The Friendly Dictatorship* that Canada can often feel like a "de facto one-party state."

Canada has also put massive amounts of power into the hands of its judiciary. At the heart of virtually every chapter in this book is an activist judge. A jurist who looked at the Charter of Rights and Freedoms decided that a vague phrase such as "security of the person" denoted an unquestioned constitutional right to do drugs in a playground or obtain suicide on demand.

Having a country with a wildly centralized political system and judiciary can be useful if, say, you need to stave off a global financial crisis or want to devise a new constitutional right without having to do a lot of paperwork. But it leaves Canada glaringly vulnerable to reckless managers determined to push through bad ideas.

Dying with Dignity was able to turn Canada into the world center of assisted suicide with fewer staff than a mid-sized real estate office. A handful of Vancouver harm reduction campaigners were able to turn government-funded "safe consumption sites" into one of the country's fastest-growing franchises. A single random question hurled at Justin Trudeau during a 2017 town hall is why Canada is one of the world's only countries where a male prisoner can go to a women's prison if they simply self-declare as female.

All this change has happened so fast that Canadians have had difficulty admitting their institutions are warped or acknowledging that their vision of themselves is radically at odds with how they're viewed in the rest of the world. "It's bizarre," said Scott Kim, the American bioethics investigator quoted in Chapter One. "There's really no cultural memory or expectation of widespread accountability. It's just 'our leaders; they're good.'"

He contrasted the Canadian approach to assisted suicide with that of The Netherlands, Canada's usual contender in the euthanasia sphere. In 2013, when public concern began to mount about a rising number of patients being approved for assisted suicide on psychiatric grounds, the Dutch government responded by publishing anonymized records for every single psychiatric-assisted suicide approved in the prior year. That's a jaw-dropping level of transparency by Canadian standards. To date, the only insight Canadians have into the workings of their assisted suicide regime is an annual report published by Health Canada, the same agency tasked with implementing and defending the MAID program. All the while, Canada produces a new MAID scandal roughly every week and none of it seems to move the needle. As this book goes to press, the latest example is a fifty-two-year-old man who was allegedly given assisted suicide while on a day pass from a psychiatric hospital.[9]

"It's like people either don't know what's happening, or their view is 'well, we have a crappy health care system, there isn't enough to go around and, what can you do?" said Kim.

And that kind of apathy is pretty consistent. Canadians roll their eyes at the United States that has seemingly become inured to mass shootings but will have near-identical reactions when their own system yields a steady stream of easily preventable horrors. In May 2023, Edmonton woman Carolann Robillard had just picked up her eleven-year-old child Jayden from school when both of them were brutally murdered on the school's front lawn. It was a completely random attack; they'd only just left Crawford Plains School when they were set upon by a stranger with a knife.

Predictably, assailant Muorater Mashar had a lengthy history of committing random violence, including against children. Just a year prior to the stabbings, he randomly began punching a twelve-year-old on Edmonton's light rail system.[10] But even as the severity of Mashar's crimes worsened, the justice system responded only with light sentences, early release, and parole conditions he was guaranteed to ignore.

The case made local headlines for a few days. It yielded the Edmonton police chief telling a press conference that "the system once again failed." But that was about it. No mass rallies. No petitions. No MPs tabling criminal reform bills with names like "Carolann and Jayden's Law."

The Canadian impulse is to see these things as tragic anomalies, as unavoidable deviations from a system that is otherwise working fine: Canada is where streets are safe and where justice is served. It's where immigrants are grateful and well-integrated; it's where sound policy reigns and corruption is non-existent; it's where wealth is so plentiful that prosperity can always take a backseat to ideology; it's where health care is free and the vulnerable are cared for; to be a Canadian is to be the envy of the world.

It's a very comforting national image. And Canadians believed it so fervently that they didn't notice anything had changed until almost all of it had ceased to be true.

Notes

Introduction

1. UK House of Commons Health and Social Care Committee. "A summary of our inquiry." UK Parliament, May 11, 2023. https://ukparliament.shorthandstories.com/key-considerations-in-the-debate-around-assisted-dying-assisted-suicide/
2. Fox, Aine. "Canada's euthanasia system should be warning sign to other countries, MPs told." *The Independent*, June 6, 2023.
3. Hopper, Tristin. " 'Disturbing' Canadian euthanasia regime should give world pause, British MPs told." *National Post*, June 8, 2023.
4. Blaff, Ari. "Bill Maher roasts Canada, calls the country a 'cautionary tale' of what the U.S. could be." *National Post*, April 13, 2024.
5. Sharma, Ruchir. "A warning from the breakdown nations." *Financial Times*, May 6, 2024
6. Green, Sarah. "How decriminalisation made Vancouver the fentanyl capital of the world." *The Telegraph*, July 9, 2024.
7. Baxter, Sarah. "Canada is the world capital of assisted dying—but has it gone too far?" *The Times*, February 25, 2024.
8. Yousif, Nadine. "How Canada became a car theft capital of the world." BBC, July 8, 2024. https://www.bbc.com/news/articles/cy79dq2n093o
9. Ruttle, Joseph. "B.C. birthrate hit a record low again in 2023: Statistics Canada." *Vancouver Sun*, September 30, 2024.
10. Statistics Canada. "Are Canadians changing their fertility plans?" Statistics Canada. March 2, 2023. https://www.statcan.gc.ca/o1/en/plus/3113-are-canadians-changing-their-fertility-plans
11. Lorinc, Jacob. " 'Such a difficult life in Canada': Ukrainian immigrants leaving because it's so expensive." *Financial Post*, November 16, 2023.

12. Inamdar, Nikhil. "Is a waning Canadian dream fuelling reverse migration in Punjab?" BBC News, February 9, 2024. https://www.bbc.com/news/world-us-canada-68124559
13. Immigration, Refugees and Citizenship Canada. "Prepare financially." December 27, 2024. Government of Canada. https://www.canada.ca/en/immigration-refugees-citizenship/services/new-immigrants/prepare-life-canada/prepare-financially.html
14. Newman, Kevin. "The people we left behind." The Line, August 22, 2021. https://www.readtheline.ca/p/kevin-newman-the-people-we-left-behind
15. Pugliese, David. "Poland wants to extradite Canadian-Ukrainian man who served in Nazi SS unit." *Ottawa Citizen*, September 26, 2023.
16. Aroor, Shiv. "India offered plane to Justin Trudeau to fly back to Canada: Sources." India Today, September 12, 2023. https://www.indiatoday.in/india/story/india-offered-plane-to-justin-trudeau-to-fly-back-to-canada-sources-2434809-2023-09-12
17. Zoledziowski, Anya. "This government agency wants you to use glory holes." VICE, July 21, 2020. https://www.vice.com/en/article/this-government-agency-wants-you-to-use-glory-holes/
18. Sky News Australia. "Canada considers life sentences for offending someone based off sex, age, or race." YouTube, March 13, 2024. https://www.youtube.com/watch?v=VLgZmF0f0uE
19. Amnesty International et al. "Joint Letter urges Justice Minister to split the Online Harms Act (Bill C-63)." Amnesty International, May 7, 2024. https://amnesty.ca/human-rights-news/joint-letter-urges-justice-minister-to-split-the-online-harms-act-bill-c-63/
20. OpIndia Staff. "Canadian Cancer Society calls cervix 'the front hole' so that trans people don't get offended by their cervical cancer awareness page for LGBTQ." OpIndia, June 6, 2024. https://www.opindia.com/2024/06/canadian-cancer-society-calls-cervix-the-front-hole-cervical-cancer-awareness-page-for-lgbtq/
21. Alberta Powerlifting Union. "Women's Classic AB Records." Alberta Powerlifting Union, August 1, 2023. http://www.powerliftingab.com/uploads/2/7/0/3/27034011/women_classic.pdf
22. Phillipp (Username). "Medical Assistance in Dying (MAID)—There Are Three Options." Know Your Meme, 2023. https://knowyourmeme.com/photos/2494781-medical-assistance-in-dying-maid
23. Bricker, Darrell. "Happy Canada Day? 7 in 10 Canadians (70%) Think Canada is "Broken" as Canadian Pride Takes a Tumble." Ipsos, June 28, 2024. https://www.ipsos.com/en-ca/70-percent-of-canadians-think-canada-broken-as-canadian-pride-takes-tumble

24. Enns, Andrew and Owen, Heather. "67% agree Canada is broken—and here's why." *National Post*, February 5, 2023.

Chapter One

1. Department of Health. "Procedural Requirements—Providing Medical Assistance in Dying." Canada Gazette Part II, Vol. 154, No. 16, August 8, 2018. https://canadagazette.gc.ca/rp-pr/p2/2018/2018-08-08/pdf/g2-15216.pdf
2. Ball, Ian et al. "Organ Donation after Medical Assistance in Dying—Canada's First Cases." *New England Journal of Medicine*, Vol. 382, No. 6, February 5, 2020. https://www.nejm.org/doi/10.1056/NEJMc1915485
3. Health Canada. "Fourth annual report on Medical Assistance in Dying in Canada 2022." Health Canada, October 26, 2023. https://www.canada.ca/en/health-canada/services/publications/health-system-services/annual-report-medical-assistance-dying-2022.html
4. Dyer, Owen. "Assisted deaths: Quebec passes Netherlands to lead world in number per capita." *British Medical Journal*, December 16, 2020. https://www.bmj.com/content/379/bmj.o3023
5. Health Canada. "Fourth annual report on Medical Assistance in Dying in Canada 2022." Health Canada, October 26, 2023. https://www.canada.ca/en/health-canada/services/publications/health-system-services/annual-report-medical-assistance-dying-2022.html
6. Department of Health. "Regulations Amending the Regulations for the Monitoring of Medical Assistance in Dying." Canada Gazette, Part I, Vol. 156, No. 21, May 21, 2022. https://canadagazette.gc.ca/rp-pr/p1/2022/2022-05-21/pdf/g1-15621.pdf
7. Kirkey, Sharon. "Why are 15 times more Canadians than Californians choosing assisted death?" *National Post*, April 10, 2024.
8. Hopper, Tristin. "Canada is getting real comfortable with killing its disabled." *National Post*, August 15, 2022.
9. Wells, Karin. "Death of twin brothers fuels debate over Belgian euthanasia law." CBC News, May 5, 2013. https://www.cbc.ca/news/world/death-of-twin-brothers-fuels-debate-over-belgian-euthanasia-law-1.1334860
10. Grant, Meghan. "Calgary judge rules 27-year-old can go ahead with MAID death despite father's concerns." CBC News, March 25, 2024. https://www.cbc.ca/news/canada/calgary/calgary-maid-father-daughter-court-injunction-judicial-review-decision-1.7154794
11. Veterans Affairs Canada. "Report into allegations of inappropriate conversations with Veterans about Medical Assistance in Dying (MAID)."

Government of Canada, June 7, 2024. https://www.veterans.gc.ca/en/about-vac/reports-policies-and-legislation/departmental-reports/report-allegations-inappropriate-conversations-veterans-about-medical-assistance-dying-maid

12. Gauthier, Christine. "Veterans Affairs Committee." Open Parliament, December 1, 2022. https://openparliament.ca/committees/veterans-affairs/44-1/29/christine-gauthier-20/
13. Martens, Kathleen. "MAID in prison: nine inmates have used Canada's assisted-death program." APTN News, April 20, 2023. https://www.aptnnews.ca/national-news/maid-in-prison-nine-inmates-have-used-canadas-assisted-death-program/
14. Cheng, Maria. "'Put to death': Canada's too-permissive euthanasia laws a threat to the disabled, experts say." *National Post*, August 12, 2022.
15. Paperny, Anna Mehler. "She's 47, anorexic and wants help dying. Canada will soon allow it." Reuters. July 15, 2023. https://www.reuters.com/world/americas/shes-47-anorexic-wants-help-dying-canada-will-soon-allow-it-2023-07-15/
16. Angus Reid Institute. "Most Canadians support assisted suicide, but under which circumstances reveal much deeper divides." Angus Reid Institute. December 16, 2014. https://angusreid.org/assisted-suicide/
17. Supreme Court of Canada. "Carter v. Canada (Attorney General)." Supreme Court of Canada, February 6, 2015. https://decisions.scc-csc.ca/scc-csc/scc-csc/en/item/14637/index.do
18. Supreme Court of Canada. "Rodriguez v. British Columbia (Attorney General)." Supreme Court of Canada, September 30, 1993. https://decisions.scc-csc.ca/scc-csc/scc-csc/en/item/1054/index.do
19. Superior Court of Quebec. "Truchon c. Procureur général du Canada." CanLII, September 11, 2019. https://www.canlii.org/en/qc/qccs/doc/2019/2019qccs3792/2019qccs3792.html
20. Council of Canadians with Disabilities et al. "Advocates Call for Disability-Rights Based Appeal of the Quebec Superior Court's Decision in Truchon & Gladu." Inclusion Canada, October 4, 2019. https://inclusioncanada.ca/2019/10/04/advocates-call-for-disability-rights-based-appeal-of-the-quebec-superior-courts-decision-in-truchon-gladu/
21. Health Canada. "The Government of Canada introduces legislation to delay Medical Assistance in Dying expansion by 3 years." Government of Canada, February 1, 2024. https://www.canada.ca/en/health-canada/news/2024/02/the-government-of-canada-introduces-legislation-to-delay-medical-assistance-in-dying-expansion-by-3-years.html
22. Whatley, Shawn. "Assisted suicide activists should not be running our MAID program." *National Post*, December 23, 2023.
23. The Canadian Press. "Assisted dying law faces constitutional challenge over exception for mental disorders." CBC News, August 19, 2024. https://www.cbc.ca/news/politics/assisted-dying-lawsuit-1.7298749

24. Dying with Dignity Canada. "Mature minors and MAID: A deep dive into the issues of the Parliamentary Review." Dying With Dignity Canada, September 15, 2021. https://www.dyingwithdignity.ca/blog/pr_mature_minors/
25. Shreiber, Miranda. "The Lobby Group That Owns the Conversation around Assisted Deaths." *The Walrus*, January 12, 2024. https://thewalrus.ca/dying-with-dignity-lobby/
26. Chapleau, Liam. "Dying with Dignity Canada." Charity Intelligence Canada, August 15, 2023. https://www.charityintelligence.ca/charity-details/458-dying-with-dignity-canada
27. Mooney, Harrison. "Dying With Dignity Canada gets $7-million donation from late Vancouver businessman." *Vancouver Sun*, June 20, 2018.
28. Maguire, Robert. "NRA revenue in freefall as member dues plummet." Citizens for Responsibility & Ethics in Washington, October 26, 2023. https://www.citizensforethics.org/reports-investigations/crew-investigations/nra-revenue-in-freefall-as-member-dues-plummet/
29. Kight, Stef W. "2024's priciest Senate races." Axios, August 7, 2024. https://www.axios.com/2024/08/07/senate-campaign-2024-election-ad-spending-republicans-democrats
30. Health Canada. "Model Practice Standard for Medical Assistance in Dying (MAID)." Government of Canada, March, 2023. https://www.canada.ca/en/health-canada/services/publications/health-system-services/model-practice-standard-medical-assistance-dying.html
31. Canadian Association of MAID Assessors and Providers. "Bringing up Medical Assistance In Dying (MAID) as a clinical care option." Canadian Association of MAID Assessors and Providers, February, 2022. https://camapcanada.ca/wp-content/uploads/2022/02/Bringing-up-MAiD.pdf
32. Interior Health. "Long-term Care Resident & Family Handbook." British Columbia Ministry of Health, February 25, 2021.
33. Hopper, Tristin. "Disability groups now assuring members they won't recommend euthanasia." *National Post*, January 5, 2023.
34. Favaro, Avis. "Canada performing more organ transplants from MAID donors than any country in the world." CTV News, January 18, 2023. https://www.ctvnews.ca/health/canada-performing-more-organ-transplants-from-maid-donors-than-any-country-in-the-world-1.6234133
35. Bernier, Govindadeva. "Cost Estimate for Bill C-7 'Medical Assistance in Dying.'" Office of the Parliamentary Budget Officer, October 20, 2020. https://qsarchive-archiveqs.pbo-dpb.ca/web/default/files/Documents/Reports/RP-2021-025-M/RP-2021-025-M_en.pdf
36. Li, Madeline. "I am a MAID provider. It's the most meaningful—and maddening—work I do. Here's why." *Maclean's*, February 13, 2023. https://macleans.ca/society/i-am-a-maid-provider-its-the-most-meaningful-and-maddening-work-i-do-heres-why/

37. Raikin, Alexander. "No Other Options." *The New Atlantis*, December 16, 2022. https://www.thenewatlantis.com/publications/no-other-options
38. Health New Zealand. "Assisted dying eligibility and access." New Zealand Government, September 11, 2024. https://www.tewhatuora.govt.nz/health-services-and-programmes/assisted-dying-service/assisted-dying-information-for-the-public/assisted-dying-eligibility-and-access
39. Department of Justice Canada. "Legislative Background: Medical Assistance in Dying (Bill C-14)." Government of Canada, February 2, 2023. https://www.justice.gc.ca/eng/rp-pr/other-autre/ad-am/p2.html
40. Health Canada. "Medical assistance in dying: Overview." Government of Canada, October 28, 2024. https://www.canada.ca/en/health-canada/services/health-services-benefits/medical-assistance-dying.html

Chapter Two

1. Global News. "Trudeau says MMIWG report amounts to genocide, promises national action plan." Global News, June 3, 2019. https://globalnews.ca/video/5349127/trudeau-says-report-on-mmiwg-amounts-to-genocide-promises-national-action-plan
2. Platt, Brian. "Laval prof who wrote MMIW inquiry's legal analysis defends use of 'genocide' in report." *National Post*, June 3, 2019.
3. Global News. "Trudeau says MMIWG report amounts to genocide, promises national action plan." Global News, June 3, 2019. https://globalnews.ca/video/5349127/trudeau-says-report-on-mmiwg-amounts-to-genocide-promises-national-action-plan
4. Truth and Reconciliation Commission of Canada. "Canada's Residential Schools: Missing Children and Unmarked Burials." The Final Report of the Truth and Reconciliation Commission of Canada, Volume 4. 2015.
5. Truth and Reconciliation Commission of Canada. "Canada's Residential Schools: The Legacy." The Final Report of the Truth and Reconciliation Commission of Canada, Volume 5. 2015.
6. Burczycka, Marta and Cotter, Adam. "Court outcomes in homicides of Indigenous women and girls, 2009 to 2021." Statistics Canada, October 4, 2023. https://www150.statcan.gc.ca/n1/pub/85-002-x/2023001/article/00006-eng.htm
7. National Inquiry into Missing and Murdered Indigenous Women and Girls. "Calls for Justice." Reclaiming Power and Place: The Final Report of the National Inquiry into Missing and Murdered Indigenous Women and Girls, Volume 2. 2020.
8. Statistics Canada. "Number of homicide victims and persons accused of homicide, by Indigenous identity, age group and gender." Statistics

Canada, July 25, 2024. https://www150.statcan.gc.ca/t1/tbl1/en/tv.action?pid=3510006001

9. Canadian Heritage Multiculturalism National Office. "Annual Report on the Operation of the Canadian Multiculturalism Act, 2006-2007." Government of Canada, 2008. https://publications.gc.ca/collections/collection_2008/ch-pc/CH31-1-2007E.pdf
10. Lilley, Brian. "Government of Canada Anti-Racism Training Documents." Scribd, retrieved on January 5, 2025. https://www.scribd.com/document/501975490/Government-of-Canada-anti-racism-training-documents
11. Department of Defence. "Systemic Racism and Discrimination in Canada." Minister of National Defence Advisory Panel on Systemic Racism and Discrimination–Final Report, January, 2022. https://www.canada.ca/en/department-national-defence/corporate/reports-publications/mnd-advisory-panel-systemic-racism-discrimination-final-report-jan-2022/part-i-systemic-racism.html#toc0
12. Lau, Matthew. "Where is the evidence that Canada is systemically racist?" *Financial Post*, November 3, 2023.
13. Canadian Association of Chiefs of Police Equity, Diversity & Inclusion Committee. "Systemic Racism." Canadian Association of Chiefs of Police, August 12, 2020. https://www.cacp.ca/_Library/resources/20200915155656 1664355016_cacpsystemicracismslidepresentationaugust2020.pdf
14. Canadian Association of Chiefs of Police Equity, Diversity & Inclusion Committee. "Equity, Diversity & Inclusion Glossary of Terms." Canadian Association of Chiefs of Police, February, 2023. https://www.cacp.ca/_Library/resources/20230303102000173977290_ediglossaryoftermscacp202302.pdf
15. Hopper, Tristin. "Education is white supremacy, Toronto teachers told in official guidebook." *National Post*, February 22, 2024.
16. Department of National Defence. "Anti-racism lexicon." Government of Canada, September 11, 2023. https://www.canada.ca/en/department-national-defence/services/systemic-racism-discrimination/anti-racism-toolkit/anti-racism-lexicon.html
17. Department of Defence. "Systemic Racism and Discrimination in Canada." Minister of National Defence Advisory Panel on Systemic Racism and Discrimination–Final Report, January, 2022. https://www.canada.ca/en/department-national-defence/corporate/reports-publications/mnd-advisory-panel-systemic-racism-discrimination-final-report-jan-2022/part-i-systemic-racism.html#toc0
18. Hopper, Tristin. "What slavery looked like in Canada." *National Post*, February 27, 2021.
19. Canadian Heritage. "Changing Systems, Transforming Lives: Canada's Anti-Racism Strategy 2024–2028." Government of Canada, retrieved January 5, 2025.

https://www.canada.ca/en/canadian-heritage/services/combatting-racism-discrimination/canada-anti-racism-strategy.html

20. Lau, Matthew. "Systemic racism claims in Canada: A fact-based analysis." Aristotle Foundation for Public Policy, October 30, 2023. https://aristotlefoundation.org/reality-check/systemic-racism-claims-in-canada-a-fact-based-analysis/
21. Vansickle, Janice. "Affirmative action: Misunderstood, feared and ignored." *Windsor Star*, April 10, 1982.
22. Humphreys, Adrian. "Agency withdraws casting call for CBC show that specified 'any race except Caucasian.'" *National Post*, April 29, 2013.
23. Transport Canada. "Civil Aviation Safety Inspector/ Cabin Safety, Aviation Occupational Health and Safety." GC Jobs, October 26, 2023. https://web.archive.org/web/20231211193133/https:/emploisfp-psjobs.cfp-psc.gc.ca/psrs-srfp/applicant/page1800?poster=1866830
24. Sarkonak, Jamie [@sarkonakj]. "Today, 18 of 20 job postings at Canada's Department of National Defence give preference to women, disabled persons, visible minorities, and Indigenous people." X.com, June 14, 2024. https://x.com/sarkonakj/status/1801640157885382963
25. Employment and Social Development Canada. "Canada Summer Jobs 2024: Application period for employers begins November 21, 2023." Cision, November 20, 2023. https://www.newswire.ca/news-releases/canada-summer-jobs-2024-application-period-for-employers-begins-november-21-2023-835476877.html
26. Baron, Christian and Mota, Adrian. "Removing barriers to funding for racialized people and persons with a disability." Canadian Institutes of Health Research, June 13, 2024. https://cihr-irsc.gc.ca/e/53907.html
27. Dawson, Tyler. "Can job postings in Canada exclude white people? Short answer: yes." *National Post*, February 19, 2024.
28. Canadian Human Rights Commission. "2019 Addendum to the 2006 Canadian Human Rights Settlement Agreement." Canada Research Chairs, October 31, 2019. https://www.chairs-chaires.gc.ca/program-programme/equity-equite/2019_addendum-eng.aspx
29. Queen's University Communications Staff. "Reducing barriers to medical education." *Queen's Gazette*, July 24, 2020. https://www.queensu.ca/gazette/stories/reducing-barriers-medical-education
30. Toronto Metropolitan University School of Medicine. "Discover the MD Program at TMU." Toronto Metropolitan University, retrieved January 5, 2025. https://www.torontomu.ca/school-of-medicine/programs/md/#accordion-1729783028755-selection-process
31. Hopper, Tristin. "Black-only swim times, Black-only lounges: The rise of race segregation on Canadian universities." *National Post*, January 31, 2024.

32. UBC Student Services. "Black Student Space." University of British Columbia, retrieved January 5, 2025. https://students.ubc.ca/about-student-services/black-student-space/
33. Kambhampati, Patanjali. "My 'lived experience' tells me that diversity, inclusion and equity is antithetical to human liberty." *National Post*, July 20, 2022.
34. Miller, Joshua Rhett. "BLM site removes page on 'nuclear family structure' amid NFL vet's criticism." *New York Post*, September 24, 2020.
35. Higgins, Michael. " 'A lot of reason to be afraid,' says censured teacher critical of the woke revolution in classrooms." *National Post*, March 1, 2023.
36. School Mental Health Ontario. "Understanding Anti-Black Racism to Support the Mental Health and Well-Being of Black and Racialized Students." School Mental Health Ontario, September, 2020. https://smho-smso.ca/wp-content/uploads/2020/09/Understanding-Anti-Black-Racism-For-MHL.pdf
37. Sarkonak, Jamie. "Toronto principal bullied over false charge of racism dies from suicide." *National Post*, July 21, 2023.
38. British Columbia Ministry of Education. "Minister's statement for Pride 2023 in K-12 education." Government of British Columbia News, June 1, 2023. https://news.gov.bc.ca/releases/2023ECC0037-000856

Chapter Three

1. McKeen, Alex. " 'Jeopardy!' champ Mattea Roach says buying a home in Canada in her 20s only realistic because of game show windfall." *Toronto Star*, April 26, 2022.
2. Team Elfassy. "Greater Toronto Real Estate Market Report." Dave Elfassy Real Estate, April, 2022. https://teamelfassy.com/april-2022-real-estate-market-report/
3. Hopper, Tristin. "Secret RCMP report warns Canadians may revolt once they realize how broke they are." *National Post*, March 20, 2024.
4. *Toronto Star*. "Real Estate Classifieds." *Toronto Star*, October 5, 2002.
5. Demarco, Zoe. "Housing Affordability Reaches Worst-Ever Level In Canada." Storeys, December 28, 2023. https://storeys.com/rbc-housing-affordability-december-2023/
6. Cox, Aidan. "Priced out: Dramatic increase in house prices puts goal of ownership on pause for some in N.B." CBC News, April 5, 2024. https://www.cbc.ca/news/canada/new-brunswick/new-brunswick-home-prices-1.7162099
7. Mooney, Chris. "The world's 3 trillion trees, mapped." *Washington Post*, September 16, 2015. https://www.washingtonpost.com/news/energy-environment/wp/2015/09/16/the-countries-of-the-world-ranked-by-their-tree-wealth/

8. Canada Mortgage and Housing Corporation. "Monthly Housing Starts and Other Construction Data Tables." Canada Mortgage and Housing Corporation, retrieved January 5, 2025. https://www.cmhc-schl.gc.ca/professionals/housing-markets-data-and-research/housing-data/data-tables/housing-market-data/monthly-housing-starts-construction-data-tables
9. Hopper, Tristin. "Ottawa could fix housing if it felt like it. They did it before." *National Post*, August 14, 2023.
10. Organisation for Economic Co-operation and Development. "Housing prices." OECD, retrieved January 5, 2025. https://www.oecd.org/en/data/indicators/housing-prices.html
11. Perrault, Jean-François. "Which Province Has the Largest Structural Housing Deficit?" Scotiabank, January 12, 2022. https://www.scotiabank.com/ca/en/about/economics/economics-publications/post.other-publications.housing.housing-note.housing-note--january-12-2022-.html
12. Canada Mortgage and Housing Corporation. "Estimating how much housing we'll need by 2030." Canada Mortgage and Housing Corporation, September 13, 2023. https://www.cmhc-schl.gc.ca/blog/2023/estimating-how-much-housing-we-need-by-2030
13. United States Census Bureau. "Total Housing Units, 2020 Decennial Census." United States Census Bureau, April 1, 2020. Data.census.gov
14. Luymes, Glenda. "Too many bedrooms: Single-family zoning contributes to housing shortage, UBC expert says." *Vancouver Sun*, October 1, 2017.
15. Kalinowski, Tess. "Toronto has too much housing despite overall population growth: report." *Toronto Star*, May 18, 2017.
16. Sun, Yang. "A Visual Guide to Detached House Zones in 5 Canadian Cities." DataLabTO, retrieved January 5, 2025. https://www.datalabto.ca/a-visual-guide-to-detached-houses-in-5-canadian-cities/
17. Cyca, Michelle. "Vancouver's new mega-development is big, ambitious and undeniably Indigenous." *Maclean's*, March 11, 2024. https://macleans.ca/society/senakw-vancouver/
18. Dachis, Benjamin. Thiverge, Vincent. "Through the Roof: The High Cost of Barriers to Building New Housing in Canadian Municipalities." C.D. Howe Institute, May, 2018. https://www.cdhowe.org/wp-content/uploads/2024/12/Friday20Commentary_513.pdf
19. Chai, Howard. "Vancouver High-Rise Development Fees 2X Surrey, 6X Burnaby, Highest In Canada." Storeys, January 23, 2023. https://storeys.com/vancouver-development-fees-chba-municipal-benchmark-report/
20. Wilson, Kerrisa. "This chart shows how much Greater Vancouver home prices have climbed over the past 4 decades." Livabl, January 28, 2018. https://www.livabl.com/articles/news/chart-greater-vancouver-prices-climbed-4-decades

21. Open Council. "Development charges in Ontario and 'growth pays for growth.'" Open Council, April 10, 2024. https://opencouncil.ca/development-charges/
22. Lafleur, Steve and Filipowicz, Josef. "Toronto's development charge increase will make housing even less affordable." *National Post*, November 18, 2022.
23. Bricker, Darrell. "Eight in Ten (80%) Believe that Owning a Home in Canada is Now Only For the Rich." Ipsos, April 26, 2024. https://www.ipsos.com/en-ca/eight-in-ten-believe-owning-home-in-canada-now-only-for-the-rich
24. Stone, Lyman. "She's (Not) Having a Baby." Cardus, January 31, 2023. https://www.cardus.ca/research/family/reports/she-s-not-having-a-baby/
25. RE/MAX. "Housing Represents Nearly 40% of All of Canada's GDP." RE/MAX, October 20, 2023. https://blog.remax.ca/housing-nearly-40-of-all-of-canadas-gdp/
26. National Association of Realtors. "Real Estate's Impact on the Economy by the Numbers: A State-by-State Analysis." National Association of Realtors, May 1, 2024. https://www.nar.realtor/blogs/economists-outlook/real-estates-impact-on-the-economy-by-the-numbers-a-state-by-state-analysis
27. Nair, Roshini. "Foreign buyers account for 10% of Metro Vancouver real estate transactions in 5 weeks, government says." CBC News, July 26, 2016. https://www.cbc.ca/news/canada/british-columbia/vancouver-real-estate-foreign-data-1.3695439
28. Lee-Young, Joanne. "'Astonishing' drop in number of empty homes not occupied by 'usual' residents in Metro Vancouver: Census." *Vancouver Sun*, February 15, 2022.
29. Stokes, Deborah. "Canada's unhinged housing market, captured in one chart." *National Post*, November 10, 2021.
30. Kirby, Jason. "Real estate prices are falling, and a U.S.-style collapse could cost taxpayers plenty." Maclean's. November 27, 2008. https://macleans.ca/economy/business/could-it-happen-here/
31. McKenna, Barrie and Younglai, Rachelle. "Housing market overvalued by as much as 30%, BoC says." *The Globe and Mail*, December 10, 2014.
32. Trudeau, Justin. "Debates of Nov. 21st, 2008." Open Parliament, November, 21, 2008. https://openparliament.ca/debates/2008/11/21/justin-trudeau-1/
33. Todd, Douglas. "Eight reasons politicians don't really want house prices to fall." *Vancouver Sun*, September 18, 2023.
34. Punwasi, Stephen. "Canadian Residential Real Estate Now Worth Over $6.1 Trillion, More Than 3x GDP." Better Dwelling, November 25, 2021. https://betterdwelling.com/canadian-residential-real-estate-now-worth-over-6-1-trillion-more-than-3x-gdp/

35. Gordon, Julie. "Red-hot and rural: Canadian towns grapple with big-city-like real estate boom." Reuters, May 13, 2021. https://www.reuters.com/world/red-hot-rural-canadian-towns-grapple-with-big-city-like-real-estate-boom-2021-05-13/
36. Boutilier, Roger. "Nova Scotia's real estate market." Halifax Chamber of Commerce, February 1, 2023. https://halifaxchamber.com/business-voice/nova-scotias-real-estate-market/
37. CIBC. "Deconstructing the Canadian Housing Market." CIBC, March 5, 2024. https://cibccm.com/en/insights/videos/deconstructing-the-canadian-housing-crisis/
38. Heaven, Pamela. "Get ready for the 'great adjustment' in Canada's housing market." *Financial Post,* December 14, 2023. https://financialpost.com/news/housing-market-faces-great-adjustment
39. Martel, Laurent and D'Aoust, Carol. "Permanent and temporary immigration to Canada from 2012 to 2014." Statistics Canada, July 15, 2016. https://www150.statcan.gc.ca/n1/pub/91-209-x/2016001/article/14615-eng.htm
40. Immigration and Refugee Board of Canada. "Irregular border crosser statistics." Immigration and Refugee Board of Canada, retrieved January 5, 2025. https://www.irb-cisr.gc.ca/en/statistics/Pages/Irregular-border-crosser-statistics.aspx
41. Statistics Canada. "Canada's population estimates: Record-high population growth in 2022." Statistics Canada, March 22, 2023. https://www150.statcan.gc.ca/n1/daily-quotidien/230322/dq230322f-eng.htm
42. CIA World Factbook. "Country comparisons—Population growth rate." CIA World Factbook, retrieved January 5, 2025. https://www.cia.gov/the-world-factbook/field/population-growth-rate/country-comparison/
43. Statistics Canada. "Canada Mortgage and Housing Corporation, housing starts, under construction and completions, all areas, annual." Statistics Canada, January 16, 2024. https://www150.statcan.gc.ca/t1/tbl1/en/tv.action?pid=3410012601
44. Hopper, Tristin. "Canadian rents continue their ruinous move into insanity." *National Post*, February 6, 2024.
45. Al Mallees, Nojoud. "Government was warned two years ago high immigration could affect housing costs." CTV News, January 11, 2024. https://www.ctvnews.ca/politics/government-was-warned-two-years-ago-high-immigration-could-affect-housing-costs-1.6720963
46. Statistics Canada. "Canada's population estimates, first quarter 2024." Statistics Canada, June 19, 2024. https://www150.statcan.gc.ca/n1/daily-quotidien/240619/dq240619a-eng.htm

47. CBC News. "Feds give Hamilton $45M to build and fix 214 rental units." CBC News, July 31, 2023. https://www.cbc.ca/news/canada/hamilton/trudeau-hamilton-housing-announcement-1.6922807
48. *National Post* Staff. "Freeland on why immigration levels are high: 'Canada has the social capacity to welcome immigrants.'" *National Post,* January 12, 2024. https://nationalpost.com/news/freeland-on-why-immigration-levels-are-high-canada-has-the-social-capacity-to-welcome-immigrants

Chapter Four

1. Harnett, Cindy E. "Health leaders reject allegation 'safe supply' adds to drug deaths." *Times Colonist*, June 6, 2023.
2. British Columbia AVI Health & Community Services. "Victoria SAFER Initiative." CATIE, January 4, 2023. https://www.catie.ca/programming-connection/victoria-safer-initiative
3. Harnett, Cindy E. "Health leaders reject allegation 'safe supply' adds to drug deaths." *Times Colonist*, June 6, 2023.
4. Zivo, Adam. "Astonishing amounts of government-supplied opioids found for sale on Reddit." *National Post*, October 21, 2023.
5. Proctor, Jason. "Warrant reveals details behind B.C. safe-supply pill seizure." CBC News, June 25, 2024. https://www.cbc.ca/news/canada/british-columbia/safe-supply-seized-campbell-river-1.7234296
6. Cooper, Jennifer. "Street Crew investigations lead to substantial seizures of prescription and illicit drugs." Royal Canadian Mounted Police, March 7, 2024. https://bc-cb.rcmp-grc.gc.ca/ViewPage.action?siteNodeId=2113&languageId=1&contentId=83299
7. APTN National News. "22 Canadians die each day to drug poisoning, says new data." APTN News, June 28, 2024. https://www.aptnnews.ca/national-news/22-canadians-die-each-day-to-drug-poisoning-says-new-data/
8. Provincial Health Services Authority, BC Centre for Disease Control. "BC Harm Reduction Strategies and Services Policy and Guidelines." BC Centre for Disease Control, October, 2023. http://www.bccdc.ca/resource-gallery/Documents/Guidelines%20and%20Forms/Guidelines%20and%20Manuals/HRSSGuidelines_BCCDC_Updated_Oct_2023.pdf
9. Hopper, Tristin. "B.C. tells nurses to ignore rising phenomenon of armed patients doing drugs in hospitals." *National Post*, April 5, 2024.
10. Hopper, Tristin. "Toronto now handing out branded crack and meth pipe kits with city's logo." *National Post*, May 30, 2023.
11. Hopper, Tristin. "'Safer snorting kits' handed out at B.C. high school after drug presentation." *National Post*, May 23, 2023.

12. Hopper, Tristin. "'Safer snorting kits' handed out at B.C. high school after drug presentation." *National Post*, May 23, 2023.
13. Jackson, Emily. "Why does Vancouver have a crack pipe vending machine?" The Verge, February 18, 2014. https://www.theverge.com/2014/2/18/5421992/vancouver-crack-pipe-vending-machine
14. Palmer, Claire. "BC to review harm reduction vending machines at 3 hospitals." CBC News, August 30, 2024. https://www.cbc.ca/news/canada/british-columbia/province-review-harm-reduction-vending-machines-1.7308489
15. Hopper, Tristin. "Toronto safe injection site apologizes for offering chocolate in exchange for used needles." *National Post*, August 14, 2023.
16. City of Edmonton. "Safe Needle Disposal." City of Edmonton, retrieved on January 5, 2025. https://www.edmonton.ca/programs_services/graffiti_litter/safe-needle-disposal
17. CHEK News. "Victoria installing signs reminding people to look for hazards at playgrounds." CHEK News, August 28, 2020. https://cheknews.ca/victoria-signs-safely-sweep-695852/
18. The ACT Foundation. "NEW Opioid Overdose Response Training to Empower High School Students to Help Save Lives Including Nasal Naloxone Spray." The ACT Foundation, June 14, 2022. https://actfoundation.ca/news/new-opioids-overdose-response-training-to-empower-high-school-students-to-help-save-lives/
19. BC Ministry of Attorney General and BC Minister Responsible for Housing. "Minimal Barrier Shelter Standards, Provincial Response." Union of BC Municipalities, 2020. https://www.ubcm.ca/convention-resolutions/resolutions/resolutions-database/minimal-barrier-shelter-standards
20. Buffam, Robert. "B.C. supportive housing worker says staff have been hospitalized due to toxic drug fumes." CTV News, April 10, 2024. https://bc.ctvnews.ca/b-c-supportive-housing-worker-says-staff-have-been-hospitalized-due-to-toxic-drug-fumes-1.6842421
21. Victoria Police Department. "800–Block of Johnson Calls for Service." Victoria Police Department, March 29, 2017. https://vicpd.ca/2017/03/29/800-block-of-johnson-calls-for-service/
22. Victoria Police Department. "Firearms, Drugs and Cash Seized In Second Search Warrant On Johnson Street." Victoria Police Department, January 18, 2023. https://vicpd.ca/2023/01/18/firearms-drugs-and-cash-seized-in-second-search-warrant-on-johnson-street/
23. Lo, Michael John. "Criminals 'embedded' in supportive housing are preying on residents: VicPD chief." *Times Colonist*, April 17, 2024.
24. Island Health. "Simple, safe, effective: Island Health grant supports washroom sensor project for Vancouver Island libraries." Island Health, June 18,

2024. https://www.islandhealth.ca/news/news-releases/simple-safe-effective-island-health-grant-supports-washroom-sensor-project-vancouver-island

25. Canadian Institute for Substance Use Research. "The Safer Bathroom Toolkit." University of Victoria, retrieved January 5, 2025. https://www.uvic.ca/research/centres/cisur/projects/active/projects/safer-bathrooms.php
26. Palmer, Vaughn. "Pinning down the B.C. NDP on involuntary treatment proves slippery." *Vancouver Sun*, February 7, 2023. https://vancouversun.com/opinion/columnists/pinning-down-the-b-c-ndp-on-involuntary-treatment-proves-slippery
27. Mannoe, Meenakshi. "Involuntary Treatment: Criminalization by another name." Pivot Legal Society, March 23, 2023. https://assets.nationbuilder.com/pivotlegal/pages/3690/attachments/original/1679547073/Involuntary_Treatment_-_Criminalization_by_another_name_-_Finalized_2.pdf
28. DeRosa, Katie. "B.C. premier softens his tone on involuntary care for people who repeatedly overdose." *Vancouver Sun*, February 13, 2023.
29. Kaufmann, Bill. "Alberta opioid fatalities down to lowest toll in four years." *Calgary Herald,* July 18, 2024.
30. Postmedia News. "From B.C. cabinet to sleeping under a bridge, Vancouver man shares his story of recovery." *National Post*, June 29, 2015.
31. Read, Nicholas. "Injection site not ready for addicts." *Vancouver Sun*, September 16, 2003.
32. Urban Health Research Initiative of the British Columbia Centre for Excellence in HIV/AIDS. "Findings from the Evaluation of Vancouver's Pilot Medically Supervised Safer Injection Facility–Insite." British Columbia Centre for Excellence in HIV/AIDS, June, 2009. https://www.bccsu.ca/wp-content/uploads/2016/10/insite_report-eng.pdf
33. MacQueen, Ken. "The science is in. And Insite works." *Maclean's*, July 20, 2015. https://macleans.ca/news/canada/the-scientists-are-in-insite-works/
34. Kerr, Thomas. "Insite has science on its side." *National Post*, May, 30, 2011.
35. Kerr, Thomas. "Are supervised drug injection sites a wild idea?" *Seattle Times*, April 3, 2016.
36. Wood E. and Tyndall M. W. and Lai C. and Montaner J. S. G. and Kerr T. "Impact of a medically supervised safer injecting facility on drug dealing and other drug-related crime." *Substance Abuse Treatment, Prevention, and Policy*, 2006. 1(1): 13.
37. Wood E. and Kerr T. and Small W. and Li K. and Marsh D. and Montaner J. S. and Tyndall M. W. "Changes in public order after the opening of a medically supervised safer injecting facility for illicit injection drug users." *Canadian Medical Association Journal*, 2004. 171(7): 731-734.
38. Urban Health Research Initiative of the British Columbia Centre for Excellence in HIV/AIDS. "Findings from the Evaluation of Vancouver's Pilot Medically Supervised Safer Injection Facility–Insite." British Columbia

Centre for Excellence in HIV/AIDS, June, 2009. https://www.bccsu.ca/wp-content/uploads/2016/10/insite_report-eng.pdf

39. Marshall B. D. and Milloy MJ and Wood E. and Montaner J. S. and Kerr T. "Reduction in overdose mortality after the opening of North America's first medically supervised safer injecting facility: a retrospective population-based study." *Lancet*, April 23, 2011. 377(9775):1429-37.
40. Vancouver Coastal Health. "Canada's first supervised consumption site celebrates 20 years of saving lives." Vancouver Coastal Health, September 14, 2023. https://www.vch.ca/en/news/canadas-first-supervised-consumption-site-celebrates-20-years-saving-lives
41. Campbell, Jill. "South Riverdale Community Health Centre: Supervisor Report." Government of Ontario, April, 2024. https://www.ontario.ca/files/2024-08/moh-south-riverdale-community-health-centre-cts-supervisor-report-en-2024-08-19.pdf
42. Vuong, Kevin. "When activists twist the truth, we all pay the price." *Toronto Sun*, September 3, 2024.
43. Humphreys K.; Shover C.L.; Andrews C.M.; Bohnert A. S. B.; Brandeau M. L.; Caulkins J. P.; Chen J. H.; Cuéllar M. F.; Hurd Y. L.; Juurlink D. N.; Koh H. K.; Krebs E. E.; Lembke A.; Mackey S. C.; Larrimore Ouellette L.; Suffoletto B.; Timko C. "Responding to the opioid crisis in North America and beyond: recommendations of the Stanford-Lancet Commission." *Lancet*, February 5, 2022. 399(10324):555–604.
44. Office of the Provincial Health Officer. "A Review of Prescribed Safer Supply Programs Across British Columbia: Recommendations for Future Action." Province of British Columbia, December, 2023. https://www2.gov.bc.ca/assets/gov/health/about-bc-s-health-care-system/office-of-the-provincial-health-officer/reports-publications/special-reports/a-review-of-prescribed-safer-supply-programs-across-bc.pdf
45. MacPherson, Donald. "A Four-Pillar Approach to Drug Problems in Vancouver." City of Vancouver, January, 2001.
46. Vishloff, Jennifer Nicole. "Striving for Connection: A Phenomenological Examination of Nurses' Experience Supervising the Injection of Illicit Drugs." Simon Fraser University, August 4, 2015. https://summit.sfu.ca/item/15660
47. Riley, Tara. "Harm reduction gone rogue: I worked at a safe injection site and it was disturbing." *National Post*, November 30, 2023.
48. Vancouver Coastal Health. "Canada's first supervised consumption site celebrates 20 years of saving lives." Vancouver Coastal Health, September 14, 2023. https://www.vch.ca/en/news/canadas-first-supervised-consumption-site-celebrates-20-years-saving-lives
49. von Stackelberg, Marina. "National ban on vaping flavours coming 'soon,' says addictions minister." CBC News, October 20, 2024. https://www.cbc.ca/news/politics/vaping-flavour-ban-saks-1.7355945

50. Dubinski, Kate. "As Ontario expands booze sales, public health officials urge caution and stricter rules." CBC News, July 19, 2024. https://www.cbc.ca/news/canada/london/as-ontario-expands-booze-sales-public-health-officials-urge-caution-and-stricter-rules-1.7268202
51. Association of Local Public Health Agencies. "alPHa RESOLUTION A22-4." Association of Local Public Health Agencies, June 21, 2022. https://cdn.ymaws.com/www.alphaweb.org/resource/collection/9DD68D5D-CEFD-443B-B2B5-E76AE0CC6FCB/A22-4_Drug_Poisoning_Crisis.pdf

Chapter Five

1. BC Human Rights Tribunal. "Yaniv v. Various Waxing Salons." Justice Centre for Constitutional Freedoms, October 22, 2019. https://www.jccf.ca/wp-content/uploads/2019/10/222_Yaniv_v_Various_Waxing_Salons_No_2_2019_BCHRT_222.pdf
2. *National Post* Staff, "Rights centre says trans activist Jessica Yaniv has filed new complaint against B.C. salon over waxing refusal." *National Post*, January 7, 2020.
3. Staff Writer. "Transgender activist organizes topless swim session for 12-year-olds, 'no parents allowed.'" Caldron Pool, July 23, 2019. https://caldronpool.com/transgender-activist-organizes-topless-swim-session-for-12-year-olds-no-parents-allowed/
4. Fonrouge, Gabrielle. "Transgender woman sues after being refused by beauty pageant." *New York Post*, October 27, 2020.
5. Small, Reid. "Transgender activist Yaniv found guilty of assaulting journalist." Western Standard, May 26, 2022. https://www.westernstandard.news/bc/watch-transgender-activist-yaniv-found-guilty-of-assaulting-journalist/article_f6c746be-dd34-11ec-932e-4bf58217e946.html
6. Eappen, Roy and Les, J. Edward and Kingsbury, Ian. "Teenagers, Children, and Gender Transition Policy: A Comparison of Transgender Medical Policy for Minors in Canada, the United States, and Europe." Aristotle Foundation for Public Policy, July 29, 2024. https://aristotlefoundation.org/study/comparing-teenagers-children-and-gender-transition-policy-in-canada-the-united-states-and-europe/
7. Warmington, Joe. "Halton school board prepares for backlash over trans high school teacher." *Toronto Sun*, September 17, 2022.
8. Rocca, Ryan. "School board aware of possible protests over Oakville teacher's attire as dress code under review." Global News, September 23, 2022. https://globalnews.ca/news/9151189/school-board-aware-protests-oakville-teacher-controversy/

9. Kennedy, John. R. "EXCLUSIVE: Trans teacher Kayla Lemieux shows up dressed as a MAN with no Z-cup breasts on first day of school as it's learned he now identifies as male and uses real name 'Kerry.'" *Daily Mail*, September 6, 2023. https://www.dailymail.co.uk/news/article-12487171/Trans-teacher-Kayla-Lemieux-shows-MAN-day-classes-new-Ontario-school.html
10. Morphet, Jack and Klein, Melissa and Golding, Bruce. "Canadian teacher with size Z breasts Kayla Lemieux spectacularly claims they're real." *New York Post*, February 19, 2023.
11. Campbell, Denis. Gentleman, Amelia. Vinter, Robin. "Thousands of children unsure of gender identity 'let down by NHS', report finds." *The Guardian*, April 10, 2024.
12. Campbell, Denis. Gentleman, Amelia. Vinter, Robin. "Thousands of children unsure of gender identity 'let down by NHS', report finds." *The Guardian*, April 10, 2024.
13. Bell, David. "The Cass review of gender identity services marks a return to reason and evidence—it must be defended." *The Guardian*, April 26, 2024.
14. Barnes, Hannah. "The Cass Review into children's gender care should shame us all." *The New Statesman*, April 10, 2024. https://www.newstatesman.com/politics/health/2024/04/the-cass-review-into-childrens-gender-care-should-shame-us-all
15. Hopper, Tristin. "Canadian Paediatric Society vows to continue prescribing puberty-blockers." *National Post*, October 17, 2024.
16. Vandermorris, Ashley and Metzger, Daniel. "An affirming approach to caring for transgender and gender-diverse youth." The Canadian Paediatric Society.,June 20, 2023. https://cps.ca/en/documents/position/an-affirming-approach-to-caring-for-transgender-and-gender-diverse-youth
17. Correctional Service Canada. "Commissioner's directive 100: Gender diverse offenders." Government of Canada, October 13, 2023. https://www.canada.ca/en/correctional-service/corporate/acts-regulations-policy/commissioners-directives/100.html
18. MacDonald, Shanna Farrell. Smeth, Angela. Cram, Sarah. Garrel, Sophia. Derkzen, Dena. "Examination of Gender Diverse Offenders." Correctional Service of Canada, 2022. https://publications.gc.ca/collections/collection_2022/scc-csc/PS83-3-442-eng.pdf
19. Hunter, Brad. "Transgender killer in women's prison had sex with victim's corpse." *Toronto Sun*, September 22, 2022.
20. Hopper, Tristin. "Alberta man legally changes sex for cheaper car insurance: 'I didn't feel like getting screwed over any more'" *National Post*, July 26, 2018.
21. Hopper, Tristin. "Canada's oldest rape crisis centre stripped of city funding for refusing to accept trans women." *National Post*, March 18, 2019.

22. Nicklas, Sharon. "Notice to the Profession and Public: Pronouns for Lawyers and Parties." Ontario Court of Justice, retrieved January 5, 2025. https://www.ontariocourts.ca/ocj/files/docs/OCJ-Notice-Pronouns.pdf
23. Employment and Social Development Canada. "Requirements for employers to provide menstrual products in federally regulated workplaces." Government of Canada, November 15, 2023. https://www.canada.ca/en/employment-social-development/services/health-safety/reports/employer-requirements-workplace-menstrual-products.html
24. Reduxx and The Publica. "Metro Vancouver Transit Police Say They 'Don't Know' Whether Sexual Assault Suspect Is Male Or Female Despite Having Semen Evidence." Reduxx, February 9, 2024. https://reduxx.info/metro-vancouver-transit-police-say-they-dont-know-whether-sexual-assault-suspect-is-male-or-female-despite-having-semen-evidence/
25. Victoria Police Department. "Have You Seen Missing Person Kevin 'Bear' Henry?" Victoria Police Department, December 15, 2021. https://vicpd.ca/2021/12/15/have-you-seen-missing-person-kevin-bear-henry/
26. Department of Justice. "Legistics Gender-inclusive Language." Government of Canada, February 27, 2024. https://www.justice.gc.ca/fra/pr-rp/sjc-csj/redact-legis/legistics/p1p15.html
27. National Advisory Committee on Immunization. "Updated guidance on COVID-19 vaccines for individuals who are pregnant or breastfeeding." Government of Canada, September 9, 2022. https://www.canada.ca/en/public-health/services/immunization/national-advisory-committee-on-immunization-naci/guidance-covid-19-vaccines-individuals-pregnant-breastfeeding.html
28. Robertson, Dylan C. "How one trans woman prompted Canadian jails to stop sorting inmates by genitalia." Xtra, January 17, 2017. https://xtramagazine.com/power/how-one-trans-woman-prompted-canadian-jails-to-stop-sorting-inmates-by-genitalia-72844
29. Blade, Linda F. "Growth of Adipose Tissue Volume and Maturity in Children." Simon Fraser University, September, 1993. https://summit.sfu.ca/_flysystem/fedora/sfu_migrate/5659/b1521445x.pdf
30. Angus Reid Institute. "Canada and the Culture Wars: On gender, more than half say a person is male or female, but one-third say that's 'too limiting.'" Angus Reid Institute, September 19, 2023. https://angusreid.org/canada-culture-wars-gender-and-trans-issues/
31. Ipsos Public Affairs Canada. "Canadians Support Protection of the LGBT+ Community, but Declining Support May Indicate a Step Back in Progress." Ipsos, June 1, 2024. https://www.ipsos.com/sites/default/files/ct/news/documents/2024-05/MEDIA%20RELEASE_LGBT%2B%20Pride_1%20June%202024.pdf
32. Hasselriis, Kaj. "Harper: hero to Uganda's homosexuals." *Maclean's*, February 25, 2010. https://macleans.ca/news/world/harper-hero-to-ugandas-homosexuals/

33. Huras, Adam. "Majority side with NB premier on gender identity: poll." *National Post*, June 13, 2023.
34. Angus Reid Institute. "Vast majority say schools should inform parents if children wish to change their pronouns, are split over issue of parental consent." Angus Reid Institute, August 28, 2023. https://angusreid.org/canada-schools-pronouns-policy-transgender-saskatchewan-new-brunswick/
35. Blackwell, Tom. "Some parents object as Canadian schools quietly aid students' gender transition." *National Post*, January 5, 2023. https://nationalpost.com/news/schools-consent-transgender-gender-transition
36. Murphy, Meghan. "Are we women or are we menstruators?" Feminist Current, September 7, 2016. https://www.feministcurrent.com/2016/09/07/are-we-women-or-are-we-menstruators/
37. Murphy, Meghan. "Laverne Cox's objectified body 'empowers' no one." Feminist Current, April 22, 2015. https://www.feministcurrent.com/2015/04/22/laverne-coxs-objectified-body-empowers-no-one/
38. Greer, Darryl. "Writer Quits Rabble Over Pulled Blog." Canadaland, November 3, 2016. https://www.canadaland.com/writer-quits-rabble/

Chapter Six

1. Dawson, Tyler. "Margaret Atwood, Elon Musk call out Trudeau's 'Orwellian' hate speech legislation." *National Post*, March 12, 2024.
2. Forbes, Steve. "Free Speech Is Under Such Threat In Canada It Would Make Orwell Blush." *Forbes*, March 22, 2024. https://www.forbes.com/sites/steveforbes/2024/03/22/free-speech-is-under-such-threat-in-canada-it-would-make-orwell-blush/
3. TOI World Desk. "No free speech? New 'Orwellian' law endorsed by Trudeau government could imprison people for life." *Times of India*, March 14, 2024. https://timesofindia.indiatimes.com/world/rest-of-world/no-free-speech-new-orwellian-law-endorsed-by-trudeau-govt-could-imprison-people-for-life/articleshow/108479688.cms
4. Amnesty International et al. "Joint Letter urges Justice Minister to split the Online Harms Act (Bill C-63)." Amnesty International, May 7, 2024. https://amnesty.ca/human-rights-news/joint-letter-urges-justice-minister-to-split-the-online-harms-act-bill-c-63/
5. Rodriguez, Pablo. "Pablo Rodriguez on Online Streaming Act." Open Parliament, February 16, 2022. https://openparliament.ca/debates/2022/2/16/pablo-rodriguez-1/only/
6. Hopper, Tristin. "The extremely Canadian media that Ottawa doesn't consider CanCon." *National Post*, October 25, 2022.

7. Geist, Michael. "The Most Dangerous Canadian Internet Bill You've Never Heard Of Is a Step Closer to Becoming Law." MichaelGeist.ca., December 14, 2023. https://www.michaelgeist.ca/2023/12/the-most-dangerous-canadian-internet-bill-youve-never-heard-of-is-a-step-closer-to-becoming-law/
8. Karadeglija, Anja. "Social media, streaming services must register with the CRTC by November." *National Post*, September 29, 2023. https://nationalpost.com/news/politics/social-media-streaming-services-register-crtc
9. Payne, Steve. "That cute little baby face carries baggage." *Calgary Herald*, April 17, 1999.
10. Peterson, Jordan. "Part 1: Fear and the Law." YouTube, September 27, 2016. https://youtu.be/fvPgjg201w0?si=HIFnp8WV2M-mQqxQ
11. Peterson, Jordan. "The right to be politically incorrect." *National Post*, November 8, 2016.
12. Justice Centre for Constitutional Freedoms. "New human rights complaints on hold over Yaniv's failure to pay $6,000 in costs to women." Justice Centre for Constitutional Freedoms, February 2, 2020. https://www.jccf.ca/new-human-rights-complaints-on-hold-over-yanivs-failure-to-pay-6000-in-costs-to-women/
13. Australian Human Rights Commission. "Understanding and preparing for conciliation." Australian Human Rights Commission, retrieved on January 5, 2025. https://humanrights.gov.au/complaints/complaint-guides/understanding-and-preparing-conciliation-unlawful-discrimination
14. DiNovo, Cheri. "Excerpt: Cheri DiNovo's 'The Queer Evangelist.'" TVO Current Affairs, May 18, 2021. https://www.tvo.org/article/excerpt-cheri-dinovos-the-queer-evangelist
15. Brean, Joseph. "Rights body dismisses Maclean's case." *National Post*, April 8, 2008.
16. The Canadian Press. "Maclean's writer dares B.C. Human Rights Tribunal to rule against him." Internet Archive, June 6, 2008. https://web.archive.org/web/20080702184944/http:/canadianpress.google.com/article/ALeqM5iVIW-FxvuTumZb5jpsKXrJa0bS4w
17. BC Civil Liberties Association. "Speak Back Against Racism and Islamophobia." BC Civil Liberties Association, August 17, 2017. https://bccla.org/2017/08/speak_back_against_racism_and_islamophobia/
18. Gilmore, Andrew. "BC rights tribunal hears Muslim discrimination claim against magazine." *Jurist*, June 3, 2008. https://www.jurist.org/news/2008/06/bc-rights-tribunal-hears-muslim/
19. The Canadian Association of Journalists. "Canadian Newsroom Diversity Survey." The Canadian Association of Journalists, 2023. https://caj.ca/wp-content/uploads/Diversity_Survey_Report_2023_EN.pdf

20. Moon, Richard. "Revisiting the Maclean's Human Rights Code Complaint." Centre for Free Expression, April 2, 2019. https://cfe.torontomu.ca/blog/2019/04/revisiting-macleans-human-rights-code-complaint
21. Hopper, Tristin. "Here's the full recording of Wilfrid Laurier reprimanding Lindsay Shepherd for showing a Jordan Peterson video." *National Post*, November 20, 2017. https://nationalpost.com/news/canada/heres-the-full-recording-of-wilfrid-laurier-reprimanding-lindsay-shepherd-for-showing-a-jordan-peterson-video
22. Pardy, Bruce. "You have free speech, so long as you think the right thoughts." *National Post*, May 17, 2019.
23. Hopper, Tristin. "Ontario town fined $10,000 for refusing to celebrate pride month." *National Post*, November 27, 2024.
24. Desbarats, Peter. "How Watergate influenced the Canadian press." UNESDOC Digital Library, 1989. https://unesdoc.unesco.org/ark:/48223/pf0000084325
25. Hopper, Tristin. "Your porn is not Canadian enough, CRTC warns erotica channels." *National Post*, March 5, 2014.
26. Hopper, Tristin. "NDP bill would prescribe jail terms for speaking well of fossil fuels." *National Post*, February 7, 2024.
27. Sarkonak, Jamie. "The slippery slope reality of criminalizing residential school 'denialism.'" *National Post*, September 29, 2024.
28. Lazaruk, Susan. "Fired worker awarded $30K after restaurant co-worker used wrong pronouns." *Vancouver Sun*, October 2, 2021.

Chapter Seven

1. Brean, Joseph. "Eight police officers were killed in just seven months. Canadians are searching for answers." *National Post*, April 1, 2023.
2. Taylor, Stephanie. "OPP head says bail reform would have saved officer's life, as critics question how it will make public safer." *National Post*, September 28, 2023.
3. CityNews Staff. "Judge who released man later charged in cop's death weighed Indigenous background." CityNews, February 11, 2023. https://ottawa.citynews.ca/2023/02/11/judge-who-released-man-later-charged-in-cops-death-weighed-indigenous-background-6525764/
4. Department of Justice. "Legislative Background: An Act to amend the Criminal Code, the Youth Criminal Justice Act and other Acts and to make consequential amendments to other Acts, as enacted (Bill C-75 in the 42nd Parliament)." Government of Canada, retrieved on January 5, 2025. https://www.justice.gc.ca/eng/rp-pr/csj-sjc/jsp-sjp/c75/p3.html

5. Lazaruk, Susan. "Father stabbed to death outside Vancouver Starbucks after asking man to not vape near his toddler." *Vancouver Sun*, March 28, 2023.
6. McDonald, Catherine. "Toronto man pleads guilty to unprovoked fatal stabbing at TTC Keele station." Global News, November 20, 2024. https://globalnews.ca/news/10879033/toronto-keele-subway-station-stabbing-court/
7. Leger. "Experience with unsafe situations." Leger North American Tracker, April 11, 2023. https://leger360.com/wp-content/uploads/2024/02/Legers-North-American-Tracker-April-11th-2023.pdf
8. Basran, Colin and Helps, Lisa. "Letter to Minister Eby and Minister Farmworth." BC Urban Mayors' Caucus, April 25, 2022. https://www.bcliberalcaucus.bc.ca/wp-content/uploads/2022/04/2022_04_05-Letter-to-Minister-Eby-and-Minister-Farnworth-from-the-BCUMC-Repeat-Offenders.pdf?utm_source=mailpoet&utm_medium=email&utm_campaign=urban-mayors-plead-with-ndp-to-do-something-about-prolific-offenders_811
9. Howell, Mike. "VPD: mental health contributing factor in 73 per cent of 'stranger assaults' in Vancouver." Vancouver Is Awesome, July 19, 2022. https://www.vancouverisawesome.com/local-news/police-mental-health-factor-stranger-assaults-vancouver-bc-5599640
10. Hopper, Tristin. "Easy bail policies make 'much of our work pointless,' Canadian police chiefs warn." *National Post*, April 5, 2023.
11. Vancouver Police Department. "Repeat offender back in custody after VPD arrest." Vancouver Police Department, October 18, 2022. https://vpd.ca/news/2022/10/18/repeat-offender-back-in-custody-after-vpd-arrest/
12. Yousif, Nadine. "How Canada became a car theft capital of the world." BBC, July 8, 2024. https://www.bbc.com/news/articles/cy79dq2n093o
13. Major, Darren. "Justice minister's government car stolen for the third time in as many years." CBC News, February 8, 2024. https://www.cbc.ca/news/politics/justice-minister-car-stolen-third-time-1.7109562
14. Fanfair, Ron. "Combatting Carjacking and Auto Theft." Toronto Police Service, June 25, 2024. https://www.tps.ca/media-centre/stories/combatting-carjacking-and-auto-theft/
15. Warmington, Joe. "Peel Region's 'Porsche Girl' gets bail twice in two days." *Toronto Sun*, September 24, 2024.
16. Pugliese, David. "Lortie pleads to be allowed a new start." *Ottawa Citizen*, January 5, 1995.
17. House, Tina. "'A slap in the face': Serial killer moved to medium security." APTN News, March 12, 2019. https://www.aptnnews.ca/national-news/a-slap-in-the-face-serial-killer-moved-to-medium-security/
18. Nafekh, Mark and Flight, Jillian. "A review and estimate of time spent in prison by offenders sentenced for murder." Correctional Service of Canada, November, 2002. https://publications.gc.ca/collections/collection_2011/scc-csc/PS83-6-27-eng.pdf

19. Hixt, Nancy. "Pedophile, child killer Harold Smeltzer admits to being 'attracted' to underage girl while on day parole." Global News, October 12, 2017. https://globalnews.ca/news/3800504/pedophile-child-killer-harold-smeltzer-admits-to-being-attracted-to-underage-girl-while-on-day-parole/
20. Department of Justice. "Rooting out systemic racism is key to a fair and effective justice system." Government of Canada, December 7, 2021. https://www.canada.ca/en/department-justice/news/2021/12/rooting-out-systemic-racism-is-key-to-a-fair-and-effective-justice-system.html
21. Department of Justice. "Bill C-5: Mandatory Minimum Penalties to be repealed." Government of Canada, December, 2021. https://www.canada.ca/en/department-justice/news/2021/12/mandatory-minimum-penalties-to-be-repealed.html
22. World Prison Brief. "Prison population total, United States." World Prison Brief, retrieved of January 5, 2025. https://www.prisonstudies.org/country/united-states-america
23. Walmsley, Roy. "World Prison Population List, Eleventh Edition." World Prison Brief, October, 2015. https://www.prisonstudies.org/sites/default/files/resources/downloads/world_prison_population_list_11th_edition_0.pdf
24. Parole Board of Canada. "Moving Towards Diversity, Equity and Inclusion: Working Group on Diversity and Systemic Racism Report." Government of Canada, June, 2022. https://www.canada.ca/en/parole-board/corporate/publications-and-forms/moving-towards-diversity-equity-inclusion.html
25. Sarkonak, Jamie. "Canada's criminal sentencing discounts for non-citizens are unfair." *National Post*, May 6, 2024.
26. BC Prosecution Service. "BC Prosecution Service releases preliminary bail data." Province of BC, April 24, 2023. https://www2.gov.bc.ca/assets/gov/law-crime-and-justice/criminal-justice/prosecution-service/media-statements/2023/23-08-bcps-releases-preliminary-bail-statistics.pdf
27. Rankin, Murray. "Debates of Nov. 28th, 2018." Open Parliament, November, 28, 2018. https://openparliament.ca/debates/2018/11/28/murray-rankin-1/
28. DeRosa, Katie. "Changes to federal bail law needed to curb increase in attack on people by strangers, says B.C. minister." *Vancouver Sun*, October 12, 2022.
29. Provincial Court of British Columbia. "R. v. Legault." CanLII, January 30, 2024. https://www.canlii.org/en/bc/bcpc/doc/2024/2024bcpc29/2024bcpc29.html
30. Forrest, Maura. "All you need to know about the Aboriginal healing lodge where Tori Stafford's killer is now living." *National Post*, September 26, 2018.
31. Clark, Scott. "Overrepresentation of Indigenous People in the Canadian Criminal Justice System: Causes and Responses." Department of Justice, January 20, 2023. https://www.justice.gc.ca/eng/rp-pr/jr/oip-cjs/p3.html

32. Department of Justice. "Spotlight on Gladue: Challenges, Experiences, and Possibilities in Canada's Criminal Justice System." Government of Canada, September, 2017. https://www.justice.gc.ca/eng/rp-pr/jr/gladue/p3.html
33. Hopper, Tristin. "First Nations getting tough on crime where feds won't." *National Post*, September 19, 2023.
34. Kerr, Lisa. "Saskatchewan stabbings: Why Myles Sanderson was granted statutory release." *Queen's Gazette*, September 14, 2022. https://www.queensu.ca/gazette/stories/saskatchewan-stabbings-why-myles-sanderson-was-granted-statutory-release
35. Assembly of First Nations. "Assembly of First Nations 2022 National Justice Forum Report." Assembly of First Nations, April 7, 2022. https://afn.bynder.com/m/560f7d60ceb81807/original/AFN2022-National-Justice-Forum.pdf
36. McAdam, Bre. "Saskatoon killer Kenneth Mackay's parole suspended after arrest in Victoria." *Saskatoon StarPhoenix*, September 7, 2023.
37. Martens, Kathleen. "Winnipeg serial murders hit their communities hard: Manitoba chiefs." APTN News, August 30, 2024. https://www.aptnnews.ca/national-news/winnipeg-serial-murders-hit-their-communities-hard-manitoba-chiefs/

Chapter Eight

1. Pritchard, Dean. "ER staff didn't believe Brian Sinclair was dead, even when other patients told them." *Winnipeg Sun,* August 28, 2013.
2. Provincial Implementation Team. "The Provincial Implementation Team Report on the Recommendations of the Brian Sinclair Inquest Report." Government of Manitoba, March 12, 2015. https://www.gov.mb.ca/health/documents/bsi_report.pdf
3. Malone, Kelly Geraldine. "Family of Brian Sinclair, who died during 34-hour ER wait, says racism still an issue." CBC News, September 21, 2018. https://www.cbc.ca/news/canada/manitoba/emergency-room-wait-brian-sinclair-racism-1.4832755
4. Culbert, Lori and Fumano, Dan. "North Van patient dies after two days stuck in waiting room of overcrowded, understaffed hospital." *Vancouver Sun,* July 21, 2022.
5. Pottie, Erin. "Family says Cape Breton woman died after not getting help at emergency ward during 7-hour wait." CBC News, January 12, 2023. https://www.cbc.ca/news/canada/nova-scotia/hospital-death-er-cape-breton-healthcare-1.6712171
6. Culbert, Lori and Fumano, Dan. "North Van patient dies after two days stuck in waiting room of overcrowded, understaffed hospital." *Vancouver Sun*, July 21, 2022.

7. Lau, Rachel. "2 patients die in ER waiting room of hospital on Montreal's South Shore." CTV News, December 5, 2023. https://montreal.ctvnews.ca/2-patients-die-in-er-waiting-room-of-hospital-on-montreal-s-south-shore-1.6673959
8. Merritt Herald. "Merritt hospital ER to close Sunday evening, marking ninth closure this year." *Merritt Herald,* August 11, 2024. https://www.merrittherald.com/merritt-hospital-er-to-close-sunday-evening-marking-ninth-closure-this-year/
9. Little, Simon. "Woman dies of heart attack in Ashcroft, B.C. after ER closed, ambulance unavailable." Global News, July 19, 2022. https://globalnews.ca/news/9002563/woman-dies-heart-attack-ashcroft-bc-er-closed/
10. Wilson, Carla. "Central Saanich seniors without a family doctor turn to newspaper ad to get prescriptions filled." *Times Colonist,* August 3, 2022.
11. Cecere, David. "New study finds 45,000 deaths annually linked to lack of health coverage." *The Harvard Gazette,* September 17, 2009. https://news.harvard.edu/gazette/story/2009/09/new-study-finds-45000-deaths-annually-linked-to-lack-of-health-coverage/
12. Second Street. "Waitlist Deaths at Five-Year High." SecondStreet.org., December 6, 2023. https://secondstreet.org/2023/12/06/waitlist-deaths-at-five-year-high/
13. BC Ministry of Health. "Cancer patients will have faster access to radiation treatment." Province of BC, May 15, 2023. http://www.bccancer.bc.ca/about/news-stories/stories/cancer-patients-will-have-faster-access-to-radiation-treatment
14. Organisation for Economic Co-operation and Development. "Hospital beds." OECD, retrieved January 5, 2025. https://www.oecd.org/en/data/indicators/hospital-beds.html
15. Organisation for Economic Co-operation and Development. "Hospital beds." OECD, retrieved January 5, 2025. https://www.oecd.org/en/data/indicators/hospital-beds.html
16. Canadian Institute for Health Information. "Commonwealth Fund Survey 2016: Infographic." Canadian Institute for Health Information, retrieved on January 5, 2025. https://www.cihi.ca/en/commonwealth-fund-survey-2016-infographic
17. The Commonwealth Fund. "2016 Commonwealth Fund International Health Policy Survey of Adults." The Commonwealth Fund, November 16, 2016. https://www.commonwealthfund.org/publications/surveys/2016/nov/2016-commonwealth-fund-international-health-policy-survey-adults
18. Canadian Institute for Health Information. "National health expenditure trends." Canadian Institute for Health Information, November 7, 2024. https://www.cihi.ca/en/national-health-expenditure-trends

19. KFF. "2023 Employer Health Benefits Survey." KFF, October 18, 2023. https://www.kff.org/health-costs/report/2023-employer-health-benefits-survey/
20. Schneider, Eric C., Shah; Arnav, Doty; Michelle M.; Tikkanen, Roosa; Fields, Katharine; Williams, Reginald D. "Mirror, Mirror 2021: Reflecting Poorly." The Commonwealth Fund, August 4, 2021. https://www.commonwealthfund.org/publications/fund-reports/2021/aug/mirror-mirror-2021-reflecting-poorly
21. Barua, Bacchus and Moir, Mackenzie. "Despite high health-care spending, Canada ranks last on number of hospital beds, wait times." Fraser Institute, October 3, 2019. https://www.fraserinstitute.org/studies/comparing-performance-universal-health-care-countries-2019
22. Money Helper. "What is private health insurance?" His Majesty's Government, retrieved on January 5, 2025. https://www.moneyhelper.org.uk/en/everyday-money/insurance/do-you-need-private-medical-insurance
23. Health Canada. "Canada Health Act - Frequently Asked Questions." Government of Canada, retrieved on January 5, 2025. https://www.canada.ca/en/health-canada/services/health-care-system/canada-health-care-system-medicare/canada-health-act-frequently-asked-questions.html
24. Pacific Prime. "The Cost of International Health Insurance Report 2023." "Pacific Prime Insurance Brokers, retrieved on January 5, 2025. https://www.pacificprime.com/cost-of-health-insurance-2023/
25. Richardson, Ben and Hussain, Yadullah. "Canada needs more doctors—and fast." RBC Healthcare, November 15, 2024. https://www.rbcroyalbank.com/healthcare-financial-solutions/advice-learning/article/?title=canada-needs-more-doctors-and-fast
26. Valiante, Giuseppe. "New study says Quebec needs more doctors, as opposition smells blood in health sector." *National Post*, March 15, 2018.
27. Kirkey, Sharon. "Canada's family doctor shortage: 10 million will soon lack access to primary care." *National Post*, February 16, 2024.
28. Kirkey, Sharon. "Ontario resident who wants both a vagina and penis wins public funding for unique surgery." National Post, April 12, 2024.
29. Hopper, Tristin. "Woman featured in pro-euthanasia commercial wanted to live, say friends." *National Post*, December 5, 2022.
30. Watts, Rachel. "Quadriplegic Quebec man chooses assisted dying after 4-day ER stay leaves horrific bedsore." CBC News, April 12, 2024. https://www.cbc.ca/news/canada/montreal/assisted-death-quadriplegic-quebec-man-er-bed-sore-1.7171209
31. Statistics Canada. "Almost three in four Canadians have a strong or somewhat strong sense of belonging to Canada." Statistics Canada, June 20, 2023. https://www.statcan.gc.ca/o1/en/plus/4009-almost-three-four-canadians-have-strong-or-somewhat-strong-sense-belonging-canada

32. The Canadian Press. "Arcade Fire singer uses MVP speech to talk U.S. politics." Sportsnet, February 13, 2016. https://www.sportsnet.ca/basketball/nba/arcade-fire-singer-uses-mvp-speech-to-talk-u-s-politics/
33. Wright, Teresa. "Majority of Canadians support private options for health care, poll shows." Global News, February 6, 2023. https://globalnews.ca/news/9458260/health-care-private-options-majority-canadians-support-poll/
34. Angus Reid Institute. "Public Purists, Privatization Proponents and the Curious: Canada's three health-care mindsets." Angus Reid Institute, February 27, 2023. https://angusreid.org/health-care-privatization-perspectives/
35. Jiang, Kevin. "Canadians' confidence in public health care dropped 10% from 2021, new survey finds." *Toronto Star*, April 21, 2023.

Conclusion

1. Ercolao, Marc. "Mind the Gap: Canada is Falling Behind the Standard-of-Living Curve." TD, July 13, 2023. https://economics.td.com/ca-falling-behind-standard-of-living-curve
2. Williams, David. "OECD predicts Canada will be the worst performing advanced economy over the next decade…and the three decades after that." Business Council of British Columbia, December 14, 2021. https://www.bcbc.com/insight/oecd-predicts-canada-will-be-the-worst-performing-advanced-economy-over-the-next-decade-and-the-three-decades-after-that
3. Reeves, Richard V. Rodrigue, Peter. "Has the American Dream Moved to Canada?" The Brookings Institution, July 1, 2015. https://www.brookings.edu/articles/has-the-american-dream-moved-to-canada/
4. Daniell, Mark. "Freeland's 2024 budget to be 'worst since 1982': Former BoC governor David Dodge." *Toronto Sun*, April 16, 2024.
5. McCormack, Carter. Wang, Weimin. "Canada's gross domestic product per capita: Perspectives on the return to trend." Statistics Canada, April 24, 2024. https://www150.statcan.gc.ca/n1/pub/36-28-0001/2024004/article/00001-eng.htm
6. Coyne, Andrew. "Canada is no longer one of the richest nations on Earth. Country after country is passing us by." *The Globe and Mail*, March 1, 2024.
7. Peterson, Jordan. "Part 1: Fear and the Law." YouTube, September 27, 2016. https://youtu.be/fvPgjg201w0?si=HIFnp8WV2M-mQqxQ
8. Organization for Economic Cooperation and Development. "OECD Survey on Drivers of Trust in Public Institutions 2024 Results—Country Notes: Canada." OECD, July 10, 2024. https://www.oecd.org/en/publications/oecd-survey-on-drivers-of-trust-in-public-institutions-2024-results_9a20554b-en.html

9. Charlebois, Brieanna. "Family who says B.C. man received MAID on psychiatric day pass files wrongful-death lawsuit." *Vancouver Sun*, December 19, 2024.
10. Parsons, Paige. "Suspect in fatal stabbing of Edmonton mother and child had lengthy, violent record." CBC News, May 11, 2023. https://www.cbc.ca/news/canada/edmonton/suspect-in-fatal-stabbing-of-mother-child-has-lengthy-violent-record-1.6839217